WHITEY and MICKEY

Other books by Joseph Durso

CASEY
THE DAYS OF MR. MCGRAW
AMAZING: THE MIRACLE OF THE METS
THE ALL-AMERICAN DOLLAR
YANKEE STADIUM: FIFTY YEARS OF DRAMA
SCREWBALL (*with Tug McGraw*)
THE SPORTS FACTORY
MY LUKE AND I (*with Eleanor Gehrig*)

WHITEY

and

MICKEY

A Joint Autobiography of the Yankee Years by
WHITEY FORD, MICKEY MANTLE, and JOSEPH DURSO

THE VIKING PRESS NEW YORK

First published in 1977 by The Viking Press
625 Madison Avenue, New York, N.Y. 10022

Published simultaneously in Canada by
The Macmillan Company of Canada Limited

LIBRARY OF CONGRESS CATALOGING IN PUBLICATION DATA
Ford, Edward.
Whitey and Mickey.

1. Ford, Edward.   2. Mantle, Mickey, 1931–
I. Mantle, Mickey, 1931–   joint author.
II. Durso, Joseph, joint author.   III. Title.
GV865.A1F6   796.357'092'2 [B]   75-46625
ISBN 0-670-76394-2

Set in VIP Times Roman
Printed in U.S.A.

We few, we happy few,
We band of brothers.

—King Henry V, before the Battle
of Agincourt. (Shakespeare)

CONTENTS

Illustrations follow pages 74 and 172.

WHITEY and MICKEY

WHITEY:

If you want to press the point, I was a real city slicker, all bright and street-smart, and I knew my way around. He was a real country boy, all shy and embarrassed when he arrived with a straw suitcase, two pairs of slacks and one blue sports jacket that probably cost about eight dollars in a store in Commerce, Oklahoma. I'd say hello, and he'd put his head down and grunt something, and that's the way it all started.

It was September of 1950, and I'd been promoted to the Yankees two months earlier. July the third, to be exact, and I can be exact about things like the day the New York Yankees telephoned Kansas City and said, Tell Ford to get on his horse and join us in Boston. Later on, at the end of September, the last week of the baseball season, the team was in St. Louis when he and a pitcher by the name of Bob Wiesler came up from Joplin, Missouri, and that was the first time that I met Mickey Mantle.

He stayed with us a week, and I don't think I spoke to him once during that time. Except to say *hello*. And I know he didn't speak to me once during that time. Except to *grunt*. He was very shy, and besides he wasn't actually joining the ball club; they just wanted him to work out with us a few times because his season in the minor leagues was already over. So they called him to meet us in St. Louis, and the thing I remember is that we went from there to Chicago, where another kid named Moose Skowron met us and started working out for a few days, too.

That wasn't a bad Yankee team. Yogi Berra was the catcher, Tommy Henrich played first base, Jerry Coleman played second, Billy Johnson covered third, and Phil Rizzuto was the shortstop; the outfield had Jackie Jensen in left, Hank Bauer in right and Joe DiMaggio in center. They were so good they even had pinch hitters like Johnny Mize on the bench alongside the manager, Casey Stengel, who was sixty years old then but who seemed like one hundred and sixty to most of us wise kids.

So when a couple of rookies took batting practice on the road, nobody expected them to make a lot of waves, especially since the Yankees were in the middle of another pennant race, trying to make it two in a row. But I think Moose hit four or five of the pitches thrown to him that afternoon for home runs, and then Mickey did the same thing, first swinging left-handed and then right-handed.

In those days, the regular players weren't too fond of giving rookies extra time for batting practice. But Joe DiMaggio made them both hit again, which I thought was very funny because he particularly wasn't too fond of letting rookies hog the cage. But he just couldn't believe what he was watching, and he wanted to see if they could do it again. So they did it again.

I was twenty-one then and Mantle was only eighteen and, as smart as I seemed, I was still so awed by the Joe DiMaggios and Joe Pages that I minded my manners, too. In fact, when our equipment manager Pete Sheehy gave me a locker near DiMaggio, I couldn't believe it. I just stared at the man for about a week. He'd say hello and things like that, but I think I would've fainted if he'd said more than that to me. My version of the Mantle grunt, I guess. But, as different as we were, Mickey and I had that much in common:

We were boys reporting for work with men, we were a long way from home, and we were scared.

We were also poor. My father was a bartender in Astoria, and for a while he worked in a meat market downtown on Fourteenth Street. My mother worked for the A & P on Fifty-third Street and Second Avenue. She was a bookkeeper. I guess you'd call us a below-average-income family. Mickey says that out in the dirt-farm country where he comes from there are poor people and there are *very* poor people. Well, I was born on October 21, 1928, and Mickey was born on October 20, 1931, and we were both brought up during the thirties—when everybody seemed very poor.

Even when I signed with the Yankees in 1946, when I was still a teen-ager just out of high school, money was so scarce that I was stunned by their offer: $7,000 as a bonus and a class-A salary of $250 a month. Not that there's anything class-A about $250 a month; it was class-A baseball, three notches below the big leagues, and that was the going rate.

I remember that they gave it to me in two parts: $3,500 the following week and $3,500 the next year. I was working for Equitable Life at the time, so I took the check and had it cashed at the insurance company. I got seventy fifty-dollar bills. The next day, I called up a friend of mine named Dominick Monzalillo and we went over to Times Square. I was going to buy my mother and father a radio and record-player combination as a gift. All that money! And I could finally do something right out of a storybook—like spend it.

We went over to Vim's on Times Square, and I saw this thing in the window that cost $181. I had on dungarees and a T-shirt, but I went right in and said, "I want that one in the window. I want it sent to my home."

And the guy says, "How are you going to pay for it?"

So I whipped out this roll, the thirty-five-hundred in fifties, and I give him four fifty-dollar bills. He looked at me kind of funny and said, "All right, I have to go in the back and make out the bill."

3 WHITEY

So I waited about ten minutes and thought, what the heck's going on here? And the next thing I knew, the cops came walking in the store and grabbed me, and said, "Where did you get this money, kid?" The guy had called them up, naturally. So it ended up that I had to call my mother at home and ask her to explain that the money was really mine, you know, explain to the cops that it was O.K., that I hadn't just robbed a store or anything. She told the cop I'd just signed with the Yankees. He didn't seem too impressed, just satisfied. But it spoiled the surprise.

That's the way it was in those days when you spotted a kid who could play ball, gave him some money and took him out of the old neighborhood. You didn't even have television then to show you how to strut around or how to carry it off. You lived from day to day, and did your thing.

I was born on East Sixty-sixth Street in Manhattan, between First and Second Avenues. We left there when I was quite young, maybe four or five years old, and the only memory I have of it was this big red building across the street where they used to park trolley cars at night. We used to play a game against the wall of the trolley garage with a broomstick handle and a Spalding rubber ball. You'd throw the ball against the wall and hit it with the broomstick, and that's my first recollection of ever playing ball.

Then we moved across the river to Astoria in Queens, where they had more sandlots, and you could see the semi-pro clubs play. They had the Colonials and the Woodside Grays, and you might even get over to Brooklyn to see the Bushwicks, who usually had some guys in the lineup who were either on their way up to the big leagues or on their way back.

In the spring of 1942, it was my last term in elementary school and all of us guys used to talk about what high school we'd go to. Guys I played ball with, like a catcher named Johnny Martin, and guys I played against, like a pitcher named Billy Loes—the Billy Loes who pitched for the Dodgers later when I was pitching for the Yankees. We were supposed to go to Bryant High School because it was our neighborhood school. But the war had just begun and some of the guys figured it would be smart to get some training as an aviation mechanic or something useful at a place like the Manhattan School of Aviation Trades. It was a pretty long commute into town, but what the hell, there was a war on and everything. Besides, Bryant didn't have a baseball team and Manhattan Aviation did.

So for the next four years I ended up taking the subway back to the "old" neighborhood, East Sixty-third Street it was, and I ended up playing ball for the next four years, too. Played first base, though Johnny Martin talked me into pitching a few games in our senior year, maybe a half a dozen games in all. Then in April of that year, 1946, they held a tryout at Yankee Stadium, and I went up as a first baseman. They saw me hit and they suggested I ought to try pitching. Not that there was an awful lot wrong with my hitting, but I was kind of small for a first baseman, about five foot eight inches and one hundred fifty pounds. They saw me throwing the ball around during infield practice, though, and Paul Krichell, the Yankee scout, thought I had a fairly good arm. So he said, why don't you try pitching?

Krichell had me throw a few to Johnny Schulte, a bullpen catcher for the Yankees, and he gave me the idea of throwing the curve ball, and I must say it came real easy to me. Before the summer was over, I had a pretty good curve ball, and I already had good control. I was blessed with control, I guess; I don't think I was ever wild in my life. I always could keep the ball around the plate even when I was a kid.

But that tryout, I'll never forget it. It was a mass thing, they had two hundred guys and they had numbers on your back, paper numbers. The Yankee scouts watched us— nobody from the level of, say, George Weiss, who was general manager then—just the scouts from the area. After the workout, they gave you a sandwich and a container of milk.

Nothing happened then, but I graduated in June and spent the summer playing for this team back in Astoria called the Thirty-fourth Avenue Boys. A really good team, we'd play doubleheaders every Sunday. I'd pitch one game and play first base the other, and a guy named Don Derle alternated positions with me. We never lost a game; finished the season 36 and 0. Then we got into the sandlot championship series run by *The Journal-American*. We won the Queens-Nassau title, played Brooklyn and somebody else, and got into the finals against the Bronx in the Polo Grounds.

It was September, and I pitched a real good game up there against a fellow from the Bronx: Lou DeAngelis. This kid had a no-hitter against us going into the tenth inning. I led off the tenth with a double and Don Derle hit another double. We beat them, 1 to 0, and those were the only two hits we got.

I struck out about eighteen guys in the game with scouts watching, but the one thing that kept me from being offered a good bonus was my height. I was still too small, they thought. About that time Curt Simmons became the first big bonus player in the big leagues. I tried to follow his example and shake more money out of management, but things didn't start to break until the Boston Red Sox offered me a thousand dollars. Then the Yankees came up with two thousand, and the Giants three. At first, when the Red Sox told me they'd give me a thousand, I thought that was more money than there was in the whole world—but I still didn't jump at it.

Then Paul Krichell took me up to Yankee Stadium again for a little workout, I think it was September 26, 1946. The reason I remember the date was that it was Bobby Brown's first game with the Yankees, and Yogi Berra's. They'd just brought them up from Newark. Bobby was a shortstop then and I think Yogi caught one game and played right field in the other.

A few days later, Krichell came over to the house and this

time he had a contract; I was supposed to get a $5,000 bonus. He asked me if I wanted to go see the Bushwicks play, because he wanted to check out a couple of fellows from Newark who were going to pitch against them. I said O.K., and he asked me to sign the contract before we left the house. But I said, let's wait till we get back from the doubleheader. So we went to Dexter Park.

When we got back, my mother said—no kidding, we weren't even in the door yet—she said: "The Giants called and offered six thousand dollars." It really sounded like it was made up between my mother and me to sandbag Krichell, but it wasn't. She just said that Jerry Monti, I think it was, a scout for the Giants, had telephoned and offered me the six thousand. Paul nearly died. But he recovered and said, "I'll tell you what, we'll give you seven thousand if you sign right now." And that time, I said O.K. The next day I went to the stadium and I signed the contract: $7,000 and the class-A salary of $250 a month.

The next year, I went to spring training with the Yankees for the first time, but I didn't make the class-A club. Instead, they sent me down to class-C, to a place in North Carolina—Edenton, it's about thirteen miles from Hertford, where Catfish Hunter comes from. My first manager was Lefty Gomez, and I guess we deserved each other because we were always pulling stunts on each other the way he used to pull stunts when he was pitching back in the thirties and was nicknamed "Goofy."

Gomez had a rule that we all had to be in our rooms by ten o'clock every night, and you don't have to be a genius to see trouble right there. We tried, though. But one night about 9:30, one of my roommates and I—a fellow named Ray Posipanka—decided to go to a carnival in town: we wanted to take a ride on the Ferris wheel. You know, we figured about five minutes of that and we'd be back in our room on time. So we got on and rode for about ten minutes, but then we couldn't get off. Every time it came our turn to get off, the guy running the ride would pass us, and he kept doing this till ten o'clock. I didn't know why, then.

We finally got off and ran back to our hotel, which was only about two blocks away. We got there about five minutes after ten, and there was Gomez in the lobby. I said, "Skip, you'll never guess what happened, you'll never believe it. We got on the Ferris wheel and the guy wouldn't let us off."

And Gomez said, "You're fined five bucks each."

Years later, Dizzy Dean had Gomez as a guest on his after-the-game television show from Yankee Stadium. And Lefty tells this story—how he'd given this guy a couple of bucks to keep us on the Ferris wheel. Now I'm in the clubhouse watching the show, and when it's over, Lefty comes into the clubhouse and I say: "You son of a bitch. All these years, you never told us." And he says, "I just never told *you*."

So I say, "Give me my ten dollars back." Now he's laughing his head off but gives me ten dollars. Then I say, scoring big, "Good, you son of a bitch, you only fined me five."

Maybe that's why they call me Slick.

Getting back to North Carolina, a couple of nights after we got stuck on the Ferris wheel, I went over to the same carnival with my other roommate, a guy named Johnny Simmons from N.Y.U. We were with a guy named Eddie Ehlers, who was the Boston Celtics' first draft pick that year. Well, I got hooked on a wheel of fortune that they had there, and after a while I was out twenty or thirty dollars.

There was one black number on the wheel and about one hundred fifty others—maybe twenty browns, twenty blues, that sort of thing. So then the guy who was running the wheel says to me—first he puts $200 on the counter—and then he says to me, "Now, kid, if this thing lands on anything *but* the black, I'll give you four to one. All you have to do is get fifty dollars up, and if it lands on anything but that black, I'll give you the two hundred dollars."

I thought, Geez, there are one hundred fifty nails plus he's giving me four to one, it's like a six hundred to one bet in my favor. So I go running around the corner and see Eddie Ehlers and borrow ten bucks from him, and then ten from Johnny Simmons, and somehow I scrape up fifty bucks and rush back and say, "Let it go."

That thing goes spinning around, spinning and finally slowing down, clicking away, and all of a sudden—*phfft*. Like that, it stops right on the black. But, just like that, I grab my fifty and reach over the counter and start swinging at the guy.

Well, Gomez comes rushing up from someplace and wants to know, what's going on? And I say, "This guy's trying to rob us." I was still reaching over the counter trying to find a foot pedal or some other device that he'd used to make it stop. Then the manager of the carnival comes over and says to Gomez, come on over to my office. So they disappear into the trailer that he had for an office and—Gomez was drinking at the time, though he gave it up later—after a half-hour, Gomez comes out and announces, "Everything's on the level."

The hell it was. Nothing was on the level—including Lefty. But I still have to bail myself out, so I call up my mother and say, send me fifty dollars. I had to pay back all the guys I'd borrowed the money from. Maybe he wasn't so "Goofy" and I wasn't so "Slick."

To this day, Gomez still kids me about my life at the carnival. But anyway, he shipped me out to the team in Butler, Pennsylvania, and I had the last laugh on him: He ended up in dead last place that year.

So I went to Butler, where Fresco Thompson of the Dodgers stopped by one day when I was about 8 and 0 for the season, and later Fresco said: "That kid has the guts of a burglar"—which was fine with me. The following year, they moved me up to class-B at Norfolk, where one of the catchers was Clint Courtney, who touted me on to playing winter ball in Mexico, where I won fourteen, lost seven and got amoebic dysentery. Then I moved up to Binghamton, New York, and in 1950 to Kansas City in the American Association, one notch below the big club.

Casey Stengel was running the Yankees by then, and I'd already showed him some brass a few months before when I was still pitching at Binghamton. Our season there ended on Labor Day and our play-offs ended by September 15. Everything was over by the middle of September, and I'd been pitching really good that summer and couldn't see any reason why the Yankees wouldn't bring me up; they were in an awfully close race with the Red Sox in '49.

I telephoned Paul Krichell and asked him to go ask Stengel why they weren't going to bring me up the last two weeks of their season. They didn't, and I was quite disturbed about that. But he told me to be patient, next year they'd bring me to spring training, which they did. So in the spring of '50, Casey met me in the lobby of the Soreno Hotel in St. Petersburg and told me I had a great chance to make the club. But I started throwing too hard down there and developed a little elbow problem; then I had a bad outing in Lakeland when the Detroit Tigers got six or seven runs off me, so they sent me back to Kansas City about midway through spring training.

The Yankees had guys like Eddie Lopat and Vic Raschi and Allie Reynolds and Tommy Byrne then: a really good pitching staff. So I went on to Kansas City and pitched there till July 1, and kept hoping they'd bring me up, bring me up. Finally, we had just got back from a road trip, and Joe Kuhel, our manager, called me about six in the morning and said: "The Yankees want you to get up to Boston as quick as you can."

That was fine with me. We had a really bad team in Kansas City that year, and I remember on opening day—it was the centennial year of the city—Joe said, "Since it's the centennial year, let's win one hundred games for Kansas

City." But by the closing day of the season—they lost a doubleheader on that day—they had ended up in last place and had *lost* one hundred games for Kansas City instead.

Anyway, when the Yankees sent me the S.O.S. that summer, I got the first plane to New York, and Red Patterson and I took the night train up to Boston. Patterson was the public relations man for the Yankees, and he was supposed to deliver me to Stengel. We got to Boston about seven in the morning, and the first thing I did was call Billy Martin, whom I'd known in the minors. I woke him up, in fact, but Billy didn't mind—he said, "I've got two girls who are going to have breakfast with us." And, sure enough, when we went downstairs, there were these two girls in the lobby. One of them had been living near Billy in New Jersey, and she knew some of the ball players. But it looked pretty funny, a couple of rookies walking into the Kenmore Hotel dining room at breakfast time with two blondes, and we took a bit of heat from the rest of the players for that little entrance.

Later that day, I made my entrance with the Yankees as a pitcher, and it wasn't as splashy as breakfast with Billy's blondes. Tommy Byrne started the game against the Red Sox and, by the fourth inning, we were losing something like 11 to 2, so Casey took a "big chance" and brought me into the game. Vern Stephens was on third base, Walt Dropo was on first, and the batter was Bobby Doerr, who singled for another run. And that was my long-looked-for debut. I gave them seven hits, six walks, five runs and even one wild pitch in four or five innings, and I think we ended up losing 17 to 4, something tidy like that.

What I remember most about that game was that their first-base coach kept hollering something at all their batters. Finally Tommy Henrich came over to me from first base and said, "That coach is calling every pitch you're throwing." The next day, Jim Turner, our pitching coach, had me throwing in the bullpen and we found out why. I was twisting my elbow whenever I cranked up for a curve ball.

Later, when we got back to New York, they gave me a start against Philadelphia and I went out with the score tied, 2 to 2, or 3 to 3. A week later, I won my first game against the Chicago White Sox. It was a night game and the score was 4 to 3, with Tom Ferrick helping me out in the last couple of innings and Yogi knocking in the winning run with a double.

July 17, to be exact. Some dates I'm awfully good at remembering.

Other dates, I'm not so exact about, like that first time I remember seeing Mickey swing the bat in St. Louis a couple of months later. I don't remember the date, but I do remember the impression he made: fast as hell on his feet, with tremendous strength in his shoulders and arms, almost incredible power as a switch-hitter—and as shy and as "country" as they come.

Homesick, too, all the time. He was always on the phone calling his wife Merlyn back in Oklahoma, and he even went AWOL a couple of times just to go back home and see her. Like in his first spring training, when he broke out in this rash in St. Pete—his whole body looked like prickly heat or something. The doctor thought he ought to stay out of the sun for a while. Mickey said he thought if he got home for a couple of days, he'd be all right. So Casey said, all right, go home for a couple of days.

He flew home, all right, and he told me later that by the time he got off the plane in Oklahoma City, the rash was all gone. He thought he'd still take a couple of days off from spring training anyway, so he went fishing the first day. But it got put on the wire service because some guy saw him; it got in every paper in the country that Mantle went home and went fishing the first day. So Casey got him on the phone and told him to get his ass back to St. Petersburg. His "vacation" was over in a hurry. After that, and after my little breakfast trick in Boston that first summer, they sort of kept an eye on us.

Mickey's one of the few guys I know who got better looking as he got older. I really thought he was pretty homely when I first met him—those teeth used to stick out, and it seems to me he had a bunch of freckles when I first knew him. But he was a real country boy when he joined the Yankees that week in September of 1950 and started to hit the ball out of sight.

I never did get to meet Mickey's father: He died right after the '51 World Series, and I think he was in the hospital during the series. Never got to meet him, but I know his sister Barbara and his three brothers.

I've only been to his family's home once. Billy Martin and I went to Commerce to go hunting with him, and I think the one thing I remember about Mickey's mother was one time when we shot about fifteen quail and Mickey woke me up the next day and said, "Mom's got breakfast ready." I went out and looked, and I didn't know what the hell was on the plate. I was waiting for bacon and eggs or something like that. But his mother had cooked the quail, and it was so good I couldn't believe it. She'd made these biscuits and the quail and gravy, and being a city boy from New York, I wasn't quite ready for that kind of breakfast—a real country meal.

But when Mickey showed up in St. Louis that first time in 1950, everything he owned was in that straw suitcase. No money, no quail, none of those four-hundred-dollar suits he got around to buying a couple of years later. Just those two pairs of pastel slacks and that blue sports coat that he wore everyplace.

Years later, we were sitting around the dining room at the Yankees' ball park in Fort Lauderdale, and they had this oil cloth on the table, and Mickey said:

"This is what we used to have in our kitchen at home. We didn't even have chairs then; we had boxes instead of chairs.

And linoleum on the floor. And when it got cold, the draft would raise the linoleum up at the ends.''

You know, he used to walk around the kitchen with the linoleum curling up around the edges. He came from a *very* poor family.

MICKEY:

When I was a kid, I used to work in the mines out in Oklahoma with my Dad for thirty-five dollars a week. They were lead and zinc mines, and I was what they called a "screen ape."

You know, when everybody gets ready to go home, they blast; they blast out new rocks and stuff. And the next morning when they come back there, the miners load up a great big van that four guys can ride—hell, I don't know how much it holds—and it goes down into the mine where they have tracks built back into these veins where they do the blasting. And they fill up these big old vans, which are really more like big cans on the rails, and they come on back up. But somebody has to push them up there.

So we'd dump them into a hopper; what do you call those things that run up with rocks? Like a conveyor belt, and whenever they get up there, they've got a screen there, and there are some of these rocks that are going into the cans, right?

So there's got to be a guy breaking the rocks up with a sixteen-pound sledgehammer. There's really two of them: one guy stands there till he can't do it anymore and then he jumps down, and the other guy jumps up and starts in with his sledgehammer. They call it a screen ape.

Then I started working for the pump crew—the electricians and their helpers—who keep the air coming down into the ground for the miners. Sometimes you have to go into a little bitty hole to bring the motor up, and I did that for a while, too.

Then my Dad got me a job cleaning out around some telephone poles. You see, when you have a prairie farm, if you don't clean out a ten-yard spot around a telephone pole, it will burn the telephone pole out, and it costs you a lot of money. So you have a guy who goes about five miles out with a shovel and he cleans a ten-yard radius around the telephone pole. And he works his way back. It's a long damned job.

Anyway, I was still in high school back where we were living out in the country near Commerce in 1948, and we didn't have a hell of a lot. My mother made every baseball uniform I ever wore till I signed with the Yankees. I mean, she sewed them right on me. I was sixteen years old then, and my brothers and me would play ball out in the yard or out back in one of the fields.

I was also playing semi-pro ball for a team they called the Baxter Springs Whiz Kids—no fooling, the Baxter Springs Whiz Kids—and one night a scout for the Yankees named Tom Greenwade came through Baxter Springs. The ball park was right beside the road, and he was on his way to watch some guy play in another town. But he pulled his car over and stopped and watched us play, and I hit three home runs in that game, two right-handed and one left-handed, and one of them even landed in the river out beyond the outfield.

After the game, Greenwade talked to me and told me who he was and everything, but I wasn't out of high school yet, I had one more year of school. He asked me if I would like to play with the Yankees, and I said, *"Shit, yeah."*

But he said, "I can't talk to you now because you're not out of school, but I'll be back to see you when you get out of school."

That was in the summer of 1948, and, when I graduated in 1949, Greenwade showed up again and the Whiz Kids had a game that night. He even got me out of the commencement exercises so's I could play in the game while he watched me again. He talked to the principal or the superintendent, and asked him if it would be all right if I played ball that night because he was thinking about signing me for the Yankees. They said O.K., and I said sure, too. Wouldn't my mother and father rather see me go to the graduation instead of skip it to play ball? Hell, no. All they lived for was for me to start playing baseball. I think what they did was give me my diploma so I didn't have to go to the commencement exercises. I didn't care about going to them, anyway.

So I played with the Baxter Whiz Kids while Greenwade watched, and I think I hit two more home runs that night. Then he told me he had to go somewhere to sign someone, but he was planning on coming back through. He told me not to do anything—at least, to wait till he got back to talk to me. And I did.

He showed up again and talked to my Dad and me, and said he was going to get me a $500 bonus. But my Dad said I could make more money than that by hanging around in semi-pro ball, right around home there. Greenwade asked my Dad how much I would make playing semi-pro ball around home that summer, and my Dad figured around $1,500. So Greenwade said he'd give me a $1,500 bonus and $140 a month for the rest of the summer. That's how I signed with the Yankees.

They sent me to Independence in Kansas right away, where they had a class-D club, and we had a great minor league team. Then the next summer, it was 1950, they sent me to Joplin, Missouri. I was a shortstop and I wasn't too sharp; in fact, I was a pretty bad shortstop. I made about seventy errors.

But I hit almost .400, our team won the pennant by twenty-five games or something, and we had the best class-C team I ever saw. Harry Craft was the manager, and I remember that right after the season at Joplin, he called me over and he said, sit down here. Then he told me, "The Yankees are going to have you come up for the last week or so of the season."

From that time on, I can hardly remember, I was just living in a fog. They'd call up the rookies in their farm system at the end of their minor league season, like the last couple of weeks, but they didn't usually call up guys from class-C. Anyway, they let me go to St. Louis, which is pretty close to Joplin, and join the Yankees there. That's when they still had the old St. Louis Browns, and the Yankees were on a road trip out that way.

I met the team in St. Louis and worked out with them, but I remember there was a pretty big crowd there and I was scared even to go out on the field. I was too scared to go out and take any infield practice or anything, but Jerry Coleman and Bobby Brown talked me into coming out and taking the infield for a while. Don't forget, I wasn't so hot playing shortstop then. But I went on up to Chicago with them, which is where I met Moose Skowron, who was there for the same thing. I guess I met Whitey when I got to St. Louis and started working out, but I was still in a fog. I don't remember him at all.

I got through it all right, but mostly I was scared being away from home and working out with the Yankees, and when my week was over, I got the hell back home to Oklahoma and went back to work in the mines with my Dad. That winter, the Yankees sent me a letter saying that they were going to have the first "rookie school" down in Phoenix next February and that I was invited to it. But I kept on working in the mines, collecting my thirty-five dollars a week, and I kept waiting around, and nothing was happening.

Then finally I got a telegram one day from George Weiss saying, What the hell are you doing? You're supposed to be in Phoenix. But I didn't even have enough money then to go to Phoenix.

Anyway, Tom Greenwade came down to our place and said they'd advance me some money. They even got me a ticket to Phoenix, so I took off.

The Yankees always had their spring training camps in Florida, in St. Pete, but this one year they switched camps with the New York Giants. There was a bunch of us rookies down there for a few weeks before they opened the regular training base for everybody else.

Casey was the manager, and he decided to take me off shortstop and put me in the outfield, because Phil Rizzuto was still playing pretty good at that time—in fact, he was the Most Valuable Player in that season, 1951 it was. I did real well, hitting balls right-handed and left-handed, and Casey said he was going to hold me over when the rookie school broke up and let me stay for the Yankees' spring training.

Whitey wasn't there then, he was in the Army at the time, so he didn't see me actually break in. But even before the regular camp opened, they had four or five of the regulars come down a little early and work with us rookies. Guys like Hank Bauer and Jackie Jensen, Cliff Mapes and I think Lew Burdette and Wally Hood. Some of those guys hadn't even established themselves yet, and I remember they were teaching us to run the bases, and they kept falling down, running around first. And I thought, "Jesus Christ, these are major leaguers?"

It was at that time that the writers started writing about "the new phenomenon" in the Yankees' camp, hitting balls right-handed and left-handed, and all this stuff. But I'll tell you, if we'd been in St. Petersburg, I wouldn't have hit all those home runs like I was hitting in Phoenix. I must have hit about fifteen home runs, but the ball carries a lot better there because the air is dry and light, and you can see the ball good because the air is so clear. They just carry better there, and I don't think I would have caught the press's attention—or Casey's—in St. Pete like I did in Phoenix.

I remember Billy Martin was at that rookie school, too. I'd always heard how smart Frank Crosetti was, you know, and he was the main reason the Yankees had such great infielders and double-play combinations. One day—I was still a short-stop when this happened—Crosetti is telling us how to make double plays, and this kid is telling him how he's got it wrong. And it was Billy Martin.

I'm standing there thinking, who the hell is this guy telling Frank Crosetti how to make double plays? At first I thought he was a smart-aleck son of a bitch, you know. Then I didn't see Billy again, because he had to go in the service.

So we finally broke camp and I'm still with the Yankees. Now, at this time I'm holding out in my mind, hoping to go on with the class-C guys that I'd played with in Joplin the year before. They were supposed to go on to Beaumont, Texas, in the double-A with Harry Craft, who I really liked. I guess I really loved him, I think he had a lot to do with getting me started. When I first came up, if I struck out, I'd go around hitting things or moping, walking to the outfield, and shit like that. But Harry would get on me about it because it would look terrible, and he just finally told me I wouldn't make it unless I got out of doing all that.

"Hell," he'd say, "you're letting it affect your play in the field and you're hurting our ball team." So he finally got me out of it; not nearly enough, maybe, but quite a bit. But any-way, at the time I was holding out to go to Beaumont with him and that Joplin bunch. But finally I found myself on a train going to Washington with the Yankees and I hadn't signed a contract yet. They were telling me I was going to Binghamton instead. I was thinking, Hell, I can play as well as those guys from Joplin; I hit .400 till the last two weeks and then I choked up. But there I was on the train going to Washington and I hadn't signed anything with anybody yet.

Finally, Casey comes up to me one day on the train and

says, "Mr. Weiss and Mr. Topping want to talk to you."
And I said, "Listen, Mr. Stengel, what the hell is going to
happen? You think it will be all right if I go to Beaumont?"
Casey says, "I think we are going to keep you here," and
that really scared me. So he went with me back there to
where Weiss and Topping were sitting. I think the minimum
at that time was $5,500 or something like that, but Casey told
Mr. Weiss that he thought I was going to make it and I
should get $7,500. And Mr. Weiss said I could have $7,500.
That's the first time I found out they were going to keep
me. I'd been reading all those write-ups and stuff, but nobody had said anything to me till then. I was figuring I was
too young to stay, but Casey kept me and I stayed on the
train with the Yankees to Washington, where they were supposed to open the 1951 season. Except we got rained out,
like four straight days, so we came on to New York and
opened at Yankee Stadium against Boston. There were something like sixty-five thousand people in that stadium and it
was the first time I'd ever been there and I can hardly remember even that, never mind the workout I had the year
before.

I played right field that first game, and I remember the first
ball hit to me. Ted Williams hit one of those Goddamned fly
balls, and I didn't think it was ever going to come down. I
caught it, but they told me later that I jumped off my feet
grabbing it.

I was scared out of my mind; I was just out of high school
back in Oklahoma and I was only nineteen or twenty years
old. One of those guys that didn't smoke in front of his Dad
and that hadn't had very many drinks in his life. That first
year in New York, though, I roomed with Hank Bauer and
Johnny Hopp, and I did learn to drink a little bit. We had an
apartment over the Stage Delicatessen at Fifty-fourth Street
and Seventh Avenue, and I gained about twenty pounds that
year, living over the Stage Deli. If any of the other guys
wanted a sandwich from the deli, I had to go and get it. You

were a rookie, you kind of waited on them.

But I was still too scared to open my mouth. I hadn't really done any drinking at all; just a couple of drinks. And I remember the first time I got drunk. It was when we were living over the Stage Deli, and Bauer and Hopp asked me what I drank. I remembered my Dad drank bourbon, so I said bourbon, and they got me a *bottle* of bourbon. I used to carry a football around with me in those days, and I drank half the bottle of bourbon and I threw the damn football right out the window into Seventh Avenue.

I heard them talking a lot about Whitey and I was anxious to meet him, but by that time I'd started to make friends with Billy Martin (later, it became a threesome when Whitey got out of the service). Joe DiMaggio was my hero, and Billy used to play jokes on him and hang around with him, but I was scared to even *talk* to him, even though I had a locker near him in the clubhouse.

DiMaggio was my hero alright, but he couldn't talk to me because I wouldn't even look at him—although he was always nice and polite to me. But Billy wasn't afraid of Joe—maybe because they were both from San Francisco. Billy was a fresh kid, and he even pulled some stunts on DiMaggio. There was one in particular I'll never forget.

Billy had one of those pens with disappearing ink. Well, Joe would always come out to the ball park in a shirt and tie—I was wearing brown crepe-soled shoes and one of those peacock ties with feathers—anyway, I just couldn't believe that Billy would squirt ink all over Joe's nice-looking gray suit. I can still see it. Billy would go up there and ask Joe for an autograph and shoot the ink all over him. Joe would just say, "Damn, how could you do that?" But Billy got away with it and always went out to eat with him, and I used to just watch and ask Billy what Joe was like. And he'd say, "Shit, he's just like anyone else. All you have to do is open up when you're around him." And I'd say, "Shit, I couldn't do that."

So for a couple of months, I was still trying to find out what it was all about—and then, when we were in Detroit, Casey sent me down to the minor leagues.

I'd been striking out too much, for one thing. I was batting lead-off and was driving in quite a few runs—even hitting a few home runs—but I was striking out too much. We finished a series in Boston, where Walt Masterson struck me out like five straight times. I had gotten picked off first by Bill White, the guy who had the real good move, and this was just after Casey had had a clubhouse meeting and said, Don't get picked off first base, no matter what you do. So I got picked off with the bases loaded, and broke up a rally.

Besides, I did a few other things, and I was getting mad and losing my confidence, hitting water coolers and all. Casey called me in when we got to Detroit and said he was going to send me back to the minors. Of course, I started crying, and he started crying. You know, he was like my Dad by that time. He felt like he had took me in and brought me up. I felt like I could play because I had signs of being a "phenom" like they were saying. I could hit a couple of home runs or steal second or score from first, but I just wasn't doing it like I thought I was going to, and I was losing my confidence. So Casey *had* to send me back, and Mr. Weiss probably had a lot to do with it, too.

I went back to the minors and joined Kansas City, and the first time up, I bunted. George Selkirk was the manager at Kansas City then and he called me over after the inning and said, "Look, we know you can bunt; we didn't send you down here to learn how to bunt. We want you to get your confidence back and start hitting the ball again."

But I didn't get another hit in my next twenty-two times at bat, and that's when I called my Dad and said, "I don't think I can play ball any more."

He was working in the mines in Oklahoma and he came to Kansas City the next day, and he came right into my hotel room and I thought he was going to say, "Geez, you're all right." But instead, he walked in and got my suitcase and started throwing the stuff into the suitcase. I said, "What's the matter?" And he said, "Hell, you ain't got no guts. I thought I raised a man. You're nothing but a Goddamned baby." And I said, "What're you doing?" And he said, "Packing, you're going home. You're going to work in the mines, that's what we'll do, you can work back down there."

And that made me think a little bit. He had tears in his eyes; he was really hot. And when he said he thought he'd raised a man and all he had was a baby—well, that really curdled my guts.

Then he just threw the stuff down and said, "Get your ass on the ball. Shit, you ain't no baby, you can do it." And he just turned and walked out.

He stayed for the game that night and I got a couple of hits, and then I wound up hitting something like .360 for Kansas City—drove in a lot of runs, hit a lot of home runs. And the Yankees called me back up.

I think that speech my Dad gave me really did it. I was really ashamed. He had tears in his eyes, you know. It was the turning point in my whole life. It was really the first time that he had to do that to me. He never had to pick on me, all he had to do was look at me and I knew what was right and wrong.

LIFE WITH CASEY

———— October 12, 1948 was a rainy day in New York. Columbus Day for the Catholics, Yom Kippur for the Jews, and the day after the Cleveland Indians beat the Boston Braves in the World Series for everybody else.

Harry S. Truman was whistle-stopping his way across the country, sniping at Thomas E. Dewey. George C. Marshall was heading for Paris and the opening of the United Nations General Assembly, saying the country was "completely united" in its foreign policy, *whatever* Truman and Dewey might be saying. Whittaker Chambers was accusing Alger Hiss of pursuing his own foreign policy. Vito Marcantonio was running for a seventh term in the House of Representatives from his district in East Harlem. Tony Pastor and his orchestra were holding the fort at the Paramount with a new singing star, Vic Damone. And Ray Bolger was opening at the St. James Theatre in *Where's Charley?*.

At the 21 Club, insulated as usual from the rest of the world's clamor, Daniel R. Topping stood before a phalanx of microphones and introduced the next manager of the New York Yankees: a fifty-eight-year-old man named Charles Dillon Stengel, who had floppy ears, a scratchy voice, bowed legs, and an unassailable reputation as a clubhouse comic. He had been a player, coach, or manager on fifteen professional baseball teams; he had been traded four times as a left-handed outfielder in the major leagues; he had been dropped or relieved three times as a manager in the big leagues; he had even been paid twice for *not* managing.

In fact, when *The Sporting News* polled 151 newspaper writers on the "most" in baseball managers, these were the results: most pugnacious, Leo Durocher; most studious, Bill McKechnie; best-liked, Connie Mack; and funniest, Casey Stengel. He received four times as many votes as the runner-up, Jimmy Dykes, and six times as many as the Number Three man, Charlie Grimm, who played the banjo and was considered exceptionally funny, even by Stengel.

So, to most people, it seemed a little incongruous—maybe even a little sacrilegious—for the austere Yankees to be assigning their ball club to such an established clown.

"Most observers," recalled John Drebinger in *The New York Times*, "always kindly disposed toward the engaging Stengel, were viewing his forthcoming assignment with some misgivings. Casey's rows with umpires stand as classics, one of his most brilliant performances having occurred one day when he strode to the plate, bowed to the arbiter and doffed his cap, from which a sparrow escaped.

"Just what he plans to spring out of his cap for the Yankees next spring is a matter that gives much food for speculation. . . ."

He was a turn-of-the-century athlete, country boy and Broadway character rolled into one. He drove a taxicab as a husky, rather oldish teen-ager in Kansas City, where he was born in 1890; he played football, basketball, baseball and occasionally hooky in high school; he turned to semi-pro baseball in 1910 to earn money for dental school; he consternated his laboratory instructors by attempting to practice dentistry left-handed; he was paid 25 cents for pumping the organ in St. Mark's Episcopal Church in Kansas City, $1 a day for pitching with the Kansas City Red Sox, $135 a month for playing the outfield with Kankakee, Illinois, and, fifty-five years later, $100,000 a year for managing the New York Yankees and Mets.

By then, he often reflected with accuracy that "most people my age are dead, and you could look it up." But by then, he also had become a landmark on the American scene.

"He can talk all day and all night," John Lardner said, "on any kind of track, wet or dry."

"Every time two owners got together with a fountain pen," observed Quentin Reynolds, "Casey Stengel was being sold or bought."

"I never played with the Cubs, Cards or Reds," Stengel acknowledged. "I guess that was because the owners of those clubs didn't own no fountain pens."

He reached the big leagues one day late in the season of 1912 when the Brooklyn Dodgers promoted him from Montgomery of the Southern Association. He rode the rails to New York, checked into the Dodgers' locker room and was greeted only by Zack Wheat, an Indian from Missouri who, like Stengel, had been "discovered" by a scout named Larry Sutton and had been routed to Brooklyn through the Southern Association three years earlier. The other players in the clubhouse ignored him. So Stengel put his best foot forward and begged into the crap game that was going full tilt on the floor before the Dodgers took the field.

He was rattling the dice for his first roll when he felt a hand on his shoulder. He turned and looked into the steady eyes of Bad Bill Dahlen, who had played twenty years as a shortstop, who had earned the nickname because he had been ejected from so many games by umpires, and who now was the manager of the Brooklyn ball club.

"Are you a crapshooter or a ball player?" Dahlen asked, getting to the point.

"I guess I'm a ball player," Stengel said, finessing the point.

"Then get out there and shag some flies," Dahlen thundered.

A short time later, Stengel was astonished when the manager called to him and said: "You start in right field for me today."

So, a few hours after he had arrived by train from Alabama, suitcase in hand, he was standing in right field in Ebbets Field. Then he was batting against Claude Hendrix, the best pitcher on the Pittsburgh Pirates, the best in the National League that season with twenty-four victories and nine defeats, and a spitball artist of the front rank.

The rookie right fielder obliged his moment in history by hitting a single the first time up, then repeated the trick the second, third, and fourth times up. So he had the comforting total of 4-for-4 in his first game when he went to bat the fifth time and found that the Pirates had just switched to a left-handed pitcher named Hank Robinson. So, to the amazement of Dahlen, Wheat and the rest of the Dodgers—to say nothing of Robinson and the rest of the Pirates—the kid from Kankakee turned around at the plate and batted right-handed.

"It was probably the only time I ever batted right-handed in the league," he remembered later. "And I'd built such a reputation by that time that he walked me."

Baseball in those primeval days was not the easiest place for rookies to build reputations in a hurry. They were collectively scorned as "bushers" or "rubes," and when they weren't being ignored, they were being insulted or even hazed by their seniors. At times, they even had to fight their way into the hitting cage in order to take a few swings at the ball in batting practice.

The only cities that permitted Sunday baseball then were Chicago, Cincinnati, and St. Louis. But a few years later, in the 1920s, Cleveland and Detroit acceded along with New York, which received authorization from the legislature through a bill sponsored by State Senator James J. Walker. The last holdouts, Philadelphia and Pittsburgh, did not capitulate until ten years later, though not for the loftiest of motives. In Pittsburgh, Barney Dreyfuss had often pointed out that Sunday baseball was dangerous because it was likely to kill the Saturday gate.

On other days of the week, ball games didn't start until three-fifteen in the afternoon or later, a holdover from the 1880s, when a starting time of four o'clock gave members of the stock exchange and other businessmen time to make it to the park after work.

But public recognition was being accorded the game in high places, in ways that would be taken for granted later. William Howard Taft was from a baseball-oriented family; his half-brother, Charles P. Taft, owned the Chicago Cubs and Mrs. Charles P. Taft owned the National League ball park in Philadelphia. So the President was known to go out to the ball game when he was spending vacations back home in Cincinnati. And when he consented to throw out the ''first ball'' on opening day in 1910, he created an institution that has amused and sometimes annoyed presidents since then.

Meanwhile Casey Stengel, the contemporary of Ty Cobb, Babe Ruth, and Tris Speaker, stood on few ceremonies after reaching the big leagues, which then numbered sixteen teams from Boston to St. Louis.

He once slid into a potted plant in the Sheraton-Cadillac Hotel in Detroit to demonstrate Cobb's famous fallaway slide. But when he was criticized in 1918 for not sliding home during a close game when he was, according to his own judgment, a grossly underpaid member of the Pittsburgh Pirates, he replied, ''With the salary I get here, I'm so hollow and starving that I'm liable to explode like a light bulb if I hit the ground too hard.''

When umpires pulled rank to thwart his tricks, he sometimes counterattacked with passive resistance. He would swoon in a mock faint and just lie down on the ground while they raged. He did this effectively one day against Beans Reardon, one of the National League's senior umpires, but

Reardon then trumped Stengel's ace by lying down alongside him, until Stengel conceded, "When I peeked outa one eye and saw Reardon on the ground, too, I knew I was licked."

When another umpire rejected his suggestion that it was growing too dark to continue playing, Stengel goaded him by signaling his pitcher with a flashlight. When yet another umpire appeared to be giving him the worst of a series of decisions, he stripped off his uniform shirt on the field, held it out, and said impudently, "You try playing on our side for a change." And when he was fined fifty dollars by the president of the league for this irreverence, he reached dramatic heights to beat the fine, recalling later:

"I went down and enlisted in the Navy. I beat the league out of fifty bucks, but it wound up costing me seven hundred fifty in pay. They put me to work in the Navy Yard in Brooklyn, not far from the ball park; I was supposed to paint ships, they found out I could paint. But then one day this lieutenant commander walked in and said, 'You're the manager of the ball team.' "

When John J. McGraw, his hero as a manager, attempted to stifle him, Stengel rebelled somewhat more gently. McGraw hired a private detective to shadow Stengel and Irish Meusel, by then the two most celebrated hell-raisers on the New York Giants after World War I. So the two players simply split up, forcing McGraw's man to track one and neglect the other. Stengel, with exaggerated peevishness, then went to McGraw and complained, "If you want me followed, you'll have to get me a detective of my own."

When McGraw's Giants played the first World Series ever held in the new home of the Yankees in the Bronx in 1923, Stengel hit a line drive over the shortstop's head and watched the ball bounce all the way to the fence in deep left center field as he circled the bases. He was thirty-three years old then and gimpy-legged and, as he sort of staggered past second base and third, he was overheard giving himself this urgent pep talk, "Go, legs, go; drive this boy around the bases."

He finally slid home as the ball skipped past the catcher, and was credited with an inside-the-park home run. But two games later, he spared himself the ordeal of racing the 360 feet around the bases by hitting one of Sad Sam Jones's pitches clear over the fence. And this time, having nothing better to occupy his mind as he plodded past the bases, he artfully thumbed his nose in the direction of the Yankees' new dugout.

The only thing wrong with that performance was that the 62,450 spectators included the strict and forbidding Commissioner of Baseball, the former federal judge, Kenesaw Mountain Landis.

"I heard about that in a hurry," Stengel recalled. "Commissioner Landis called me over to his box seat and said he didn't like that kind of exhibition before sixty thousand people, and he told me, 'If you do that again, I promise you one thing: You won't receive a dollar of your World Series share.' "

To emphasize the point, Landis fined Stengel fifty dollars on the spot. But the Judge quietly refused to inflict sterner punishment, as the Yankees demanded, and theorized: "Well, Casey Stengel just can't help being Casey Stengel."

When he was traded two years later to the Boston Braves, he was installed as a "one-man triumvirate" for the Braves' farm club at Worcester, Massachusetts, in the Eastern League—president, manager, and outfielder. He fretted through his first assignment as an executive for one season. He even played in 100 of the team's 125 games, and the club finished third. But at the end of the season, he executed a monumental front-office triple play to escape. As manager, he released Stengel the player. As president, he fired Stengel the manager. And as Stengel, he resigned as president.

But he was a man marked by his own talents. He was hired

as a manager at Toledo in the American Association for six summers, in Brooklyn and Boston in the National League for nine more, then in Milwaukee and Kansas City in the American Association for two years, and finally in Oakland in the Pacific Coast League for three years starting in 1946. When his team won 114 games and the pennant in 1948, the Yankees were waiting.

He accomplished all this cross-country roaming to the accompaniment of a nonstop, marathon, circuitous style of speaking that became known as "Stengelese." It was a rambling semi-doubletalk laced with ambiguous, assumed or unknown antecedents, a liberal use of "which" instead of "who" or "that," a roundabout narrative framed in great generalities and dangling modifiers, a lack of proper names for "that fella" or simply "the shortstop," plus flashes of incisiveness tacked onto the ends of sentences, like: "And, of course, they got Perranoski."

Strict followers of Stengelese always found a meaning at the end of the trail, though often an hour later; between the layers of dangling participles and fused phrases, a point lurked. Sometimes, it was made rather quickly in short or clipped Stengelese, most frequently to summarize a baseball player's ability or idiosyncrasies or to define a situation starkly.

Of Jim Bunning, who pitched successfully for both the Detroit Tigers of the American League and the Philadelphia Phillies of the National League, he said: "He must be good. He gets 'em out in both leagues."

Of Van Lingle Mungo, his wild man with the Dodgers in the 1930s: "Mungo and I get along fine. I just tell him I won't stand for no nonsense—and then I duck."

Of ball players and their occasional lack of hustle: "I ain't seen no one die on a ball field chasing flies. And the pitchers. I bet I lost six games fieldin' by a pitcher. He's got an eighteen-dollar glove, ain't he?"

Of Willie Mays, who played for the San Francisco Giants

in windy Candlestick Park: "If a typhoon is blowing, he catches the ball."

Of a ball player with a problem: "That feller runs splendid but he needs help at the plate, which coming from the country chasing rabbits all winter give him strong legs, although he broke one falling out of a tree, which shows you can't tell, and when a curve ball comes he waves at it and if pitchers don't throw curves you have no pitching staff, so how is a manager going to know whether to tell boys to fall out of trees and break legs so he can run fast even if he can't hit a curve ball?"

Of baseball itself and the nature of the game: "You got to get twenty-seven outs to win."

For half a century after he married Edna Lawson in 1924, he made his base of operations in a large home at the foot of the Sierras in Glendale, California. But he maintained his barrage of speaking even when chained occasionally to a desk as vice president and director of the Valley National Bank of Glendale, which he and his wife's family controlled.

"We're a national bank," he once announced, "and this is what you call a subsidiary. That's correct. Our main office is over in Glendale and this is a subsiduary—a branch. You can't ask me to go downstairs and run an I.B.M. machine without a college I.B.M. course. And I'm not supposed to talk about the banking business at all, because gold is leaving the country.

"Now this is the board room. See over there on the chart—capital assets and all that. Now you ask me, if this is the board room, where is the board, and I say this ain't the day the board meets. Okay?

"Now, in there where it says 'escrows' is where they can take people in and talk about escrows, so it won't be out in public."

As a result of all his hell-raising, people wondered with total justification how he might respond to the challenges of handling twenty-five or so young baseball players when he was entrusted with the reins of managing a team. And Stengel rose to that occasion, too, declaring:

"Now that I'm a manager, I see the error of my youthful ways. If any player pulled that stuff on me now, I would probably fine his ears off."

When they finally let him take the stage in the 21 Club that day, the tape recorders and microphones and cameras were all switched on at a common cue, and the man of the hour wasted no time proving that all his press notices were the absolute truth. He stepped forward and said:

"I want first of all to thank Mr. Bob Topping for this opportunity."

Which was all right, except that Mr. *Dan* Topping should have been thanked for this opportunity instead of his brother, Mr. Bob Topping, whose marital difficulties with Arlene Judge, the film actress, formerly Dan's wife, had put both Toppings in headlines before Stengel had arrived.

Cries of "Cut!" and "Hold it!" drowned out whatever else the Yankees' new manager had in mind for his inaugural address. Then, after everybody had rewound the equipment, Casey took another cue, made another start and took another stab at it.

He was the fifth candidate in three years to take a stab at running the Yankees, a team that was already being criticized as a "morning glory." But a morning glory that promptly blossomed into ten American League pennants and seven world series championships in the next twelve years—under the funniest manager in baseball.

ONE STARE
FROM DIMAGGIO

MICKEY: ⒸＣasey used to hit fungoes to the outfielders and run the bases to show us young guys his hook-slide, and I remember once he even took me out to the fence and pretended somebody hit a baseball off it. He played the rebound off the fence, wheeled around and threw it in to one of the infielders. I guess he thought I wasn't too Goddamned impressed, because somebody said later that Casey told them, "Mantle thinks I was born at the age of sixty-two and commenced managing immediately."

WHITEY:
When I got there, I was expecting an older club because the guys were already heroes to me. Joe DiMaggio, Phil Rizzuto, Billy Johnson, Tommy Henrich, Yogi Berra—I always used to picture them as so much older than me. But when I got there, I found out they weren't. Yogi was only three or four years older than me, Jackie Jensen was only a year or so older, even guys like Eddie Lopat had at most ten years on me, and Lopat treated me more like his brother.

When they called me up in 1950, Casey was just hitting sixty that July, but he was sharp as hell. He always seemed to be two or three innings ahead of everybody else. He knew if the other club put somebody in to pitch, he'd already have Johnny Hopp in mind to pinch-hit. Or Johnny Mize or Joe Collins or somebody. Shrewd, shrewd as hell, the Old Man was.

After a while, everybody seemed twelve feet tall. You know, they already had guys like DiMaggio and Joe Page and Allie Reynolds when I joined the club in 1950. And after that, up until 1965, the only years I remember *not* winning the pennant were '54 and '59. The first time, we won over a hundred games, but Cleveland still beat us out by eight or nine games. The other time, we had an off-year and Chicago beat us out. It was unbelievable, growing up in New York and being a Yankee fan since I was seven or eight years old, then joining them and winning thirteen pennants in fifteen years. That's a lot of World Series rings. And checks.

They made you bust your ass to collect them, too. I know when they called me up from Kansas City that summer, I got paid on a scale of about five thousand for that season. Then we won the pennant and the world series and I think our check for winning came to six or seven thousand apiece. So you could more than double your money. And that was one of the things they drummed into you: Whatever you do off the field, don't fuck up on the field—you were earning money for the other guys. Even later, when I started making good money, I'd always worry that I wouldn't pitch a good game because of my living habits or something like that, maybe staying up late at night. If we didn't happen to get into the World Series, it wasn't going to hurt me as much as some of the rookies who were still only making seven or eight thousand dollars.

When Casey took over the club, some people figured it'd be a ball because he'd been such a hell-raiser himself. But right off, he hired Jim Turner as his pitching coach, and Turner didn't go for a lot of horsing around. He was fairly old himself; when he started in the big leagues, he was one of the oldest rookies around, like thirty-three years old. So things were pretty serious.

Guys like Gene Woodling and Hank Bauer would be screaming all the time because they wanted to play all the time. But Casey just let them holler. He'd have Woodling in right field against right-handed pitchers and Bauer in right field against the left-handers, and you look at their marks at the end of the season and they'd both have about 50 RBIs and they'd both be hitting .290, maybe .295. So you figure your "right field" is getting a hundred runs for you.

It sometimes took the guys a while to understand that Casey knew what the hell it was all about. But he had good ball players to work with and he took full advantage of the players he had. And I think it was sort of the beginning of platooning guys.

He had an awful good knack for coming up with the right player at the end of the season, too. The last month, they'd be coming up with a Johnny Sain or Johnny Hopp or a Johnny Mize, the one good ball player who could clinch the pennant for you.

Remember, I pitched my first game up in Boston, the day Billy Martin and I waltzed into the dining room with the two blondes. I wasn't so hot that day, but then a week later Casey pitched me again in New York against Philadelphia. It was my first start and we won the game, but I wasn't involved in the decision. Ferrick got the win when we won it in the ninth on a double by Yogi. Finally, though, on July 17th, in a night game at the stadium, I got my first win. Ferrick relieved me again in the eighth inning with the bases loaded and two out, and struck out some pinch hitter and we beat the White Sox, 4 to 3. Yogi knocked in the two winning runs that time, too.

The thing I remember about that game was that I hustled up about seventy-three tickets for my relatives and friends from Astoria, and that's probably still the club record. I went around and got them from everybody—the traveling secretary, the other players, everybody. I just kept asking them, "Can I have your tickets tonight, can I have your tickets?" You were supposed to get a pair of free tickets besides whatever you needed for your immediate family. This time, the whole neighborhood turned out, and I had the biggest "immediate family" in Yankee history.

After that, Casey would let me pitch against the second-division clubs, that's how cute he was. He'd pitch me against Washington and the St. Louis Browns, and I got my record built up to something like 6 and 0 before he finally put me in against a tough club. It was in Detroit and we were half a game behind them in the pennant race, so we really had to win two out of three to get into first place. We got beat the first game, something like 9 to 5, but we won the next game, 7 to 5, and then Casey told me I'd be pitching the next day. It was the first time I pitched against a pennant contender, but he figured that by then I'd had a few knocks and wouldn't go all to pieces.

It was also the first time I got into any kind of encounter with Casey, the one-on-one thing that becomes part of your schooling in baseball. The other pitcher was Dizzy Trout, and I remember that Joe DiMaggio clipped him for a home run and there I was, protecting a 1-to-0 lead most of the game. But toward the end of it, Vic Wertz and George Kell hit back-to-back doubles off me to tie the score. There was a man on second, one run in and nobody out, and there comes old Casey strolling toward the mound—I was really afraid he was going to take me out.

The first thing he asked me was: Are you tired? And I told him no, I wasn't. I'm not saying I wasn't actually tired, I'm saying that I told the Old Man I wasn't tired. What I did was talk him into letting me stay in the game, and I lucked out because the next three guys hit ground balls to Rizzuto, so the run didn't score. Later, in the top of the ninth, I thought Casey would take me out for a pinch hitter, but he didn't. I guess I was so convincing the first time that he decided to let me go all the way; or maybe he was just teaching me a lesson about telling the truth.

Whatever he was doing, I stayed in and got a walk and—this is what the Yankees were all about in those days—we ended up getting six runs that inning and won the game, 7 to 1. But I learned the lesson, all right. We had probably ten writers following the club then—they had so many newspapers in New York in those days—and so I tried to be real nonchalant when they crowded around my locker after the game. I tried to make believe it was just an ordinary game, like I was pitching back in Astoria on the sandlots. But underneath, I was nervous as hell, you know, because he'd let me stay in and the game put us in first place, and we stayed there the rest of the season and beat out the Tigers by three games for the pennant.

The thing I learned that day, though, was not to try bluffing your way past Stengel. Every pitcher wants to stay in the game, and I used to get like that, too. He'd ask if I was tired and I'd say no, and a lot of times I'd be lying, I really was tired and it hurt us, because we lost a couple of games that way. It took me a year or two to get the point for good, but I did. Later, when Ralph Houk was running the team, I'd tell him that I'd pitch as hard as I could as long as I could, and he'd say okay, just be honest with me and, if you *are* tired, let me know.

Anyway, I ended up that year 9 and 1, my first summer with Casey. Actually, I won the nine in a row, but late in the season—it was like September 27th—he brought me in to relieve Eddie Lopat against the Philadelphia Athletics and I didn't make it. It was funny as hell, because we had a one-run lead in the ninth inning and for some reason Houk was catching (I don't know what happened to Yogi, he used to catch one hundred fifty games every season and Casey would let Houk or Charlie Silvera or somebody catch the other four). But now the Athletics get a man on base and Sam Chapman is up. And no fooling, Ralph kept giving me the curve ball sign—nine straight times, only curve balls. We got two strikes on him, still throwing nothing but curves, and Chapman kept fouling them off. But each one he fouled off a little better, as though he was getting a bigger piece of it all the time. But still Ralph kept calling for the curve ball and I kept throwing it, and Sam kept fouling it, and the ninth one he hit into the upper deck.

MICKEY:

Don't forget, I'm the guy who got struck out five straight times by Walt Masterson, just before Casey sent me down. Sometimes I used to wish somebody would throw *me* nine straight somethings. Even if you couldn't believe it and even if you were guessing pretty hard that he'd switch, you'd be getting a better look at it, whatever it was. Maybe Whitey and me just went to streaks. When I was trying to play short-stop down in Independence and Joplin—the same summer Houk was calling all those curve balls for you—I was streaky as hell. The only thing I did consistently at shortstop was throw wild to first base. They could count on that. The people in Independence and Joplin wouldn't even stand behind first base when I was playing short—they'd clear the whole place out.

WHITEY:

Once I got done throwing curve balls to Sam Chapman, the Yankees straightened out and won the pennant, and it was their second straight under Casey. Then we were in the World Series in Philadelphia, and that's when I began to think the Yankees always ended their season by playing in the Series.

Talking about pitching, that was a beaut. Vic Raschi beat Jim Konstanty in the first game, 1 to 0, then Allie Reynolds beat Robin Roberts in the second game, 2 to 1 in ten innings. We got back to Yankee Stadium and Lopat and Ferrick won the third game, 3 to 2, and nobody was still hitting very much. And finally, Casey told me I was going to start the fourth game, and I had to go around scrounging tickets all over again. You know, I needed sixty or seventy tickets for my family and friends, and that's one of the times when you have to pay for tickets—the World Series—because they don't have any passes at all for the games, and I had some job rushing around getting a couple from this guy and a few more from that guy.

After all that, we had a 5-to-0 lead in the ninth when Gene Woodling dropped a fly ball—he was in left field then—with two outs and a couple of guys on base, and the Phillies scored and still had something going. So out comes Casey to the mound and this time he doesn't even bother to ask me if I'm tired. He just took me out and brought in Reynolds, and I had to admire him for that because the fans were really getting on him for taking me out with two down in the ninth. Hell, half of them were my relatives, anyway. But I'll never forget Reynolds coming in, he was the meanest-looking pitcher I ever saw and it was October and it was getting tough to see the ball in the stadium with that haze, and besides it was late afternoon and getting dark.

I was still only twenty-one years old and I'd started that year in the minor leagues, where you hardly ever talked about brushback pitches or things like that. But I was always damned happy it wasn't me swinging against Reynolds in the haze that time. It was Stan Lopata, the Phillies' big catcher, and he was a right-hander. Allie just came in and blew three fast balls right past him, and that was the Series.

I always felt bad about Woodling that time, even though we won, because I had a shutout with two out in the ninth, and he had to fight that fly ball for me. The average fan doesn't know how tough it is to catch a ball out in left field in Yankee Stadium in October, especially in the late innings with the sun right behind the stands. It wasn't an easy fly ball either, it was sort of a line drive, and I could see it was trouble—the way Gene was going after it, trying to flip his sunglasses down so he could see it. He finally dropped it, and they got their two runs, but later—after Reynolds came in and stopped all the nonsense—all the writers flocked over to me, saying things like: "Gee, your first World Series, what do you think of Woodling dropping that ball when you could have had a shutout?"

Later, when the writers cleared out, I went over to Gene and let him know I wasn't mad that he dropped the ball. Especially a guy like Woodling, you know, the way he always used to put out.

It wasn't one of those cases where a guy blows a play or a game because he came to work after a long night of drinking or bouncing around. That's when you'd be running the risk of screwing up, and it'd be your fault. When that happened, Hank Bauer settled it in a hurry. He looked you right in the eyes and sort of growled, "Don't fool around with my money." And that's one of the things that kept the guys sort of straight, the idea that you're not only screwing yourself but you're also taking money out of everybody else's pocket if you screw up.

I remember once, Joe Page and I went out one night that year when I was just a rookie. I couldn't help feeling excited that here was Joe Page asking me to go to dinner with him in Chicago. We went to a real nice restaurant, and then we went to watch the fights in a place like Madison Square Garden back home, and then we went bouncing around town and before we knew it, it got pretty late.

But Joe knew a place where they'd still let us in, it was called the Airline Club or something. The front door was closed, but Joe knocked on the window, and the owner comes to it and looks out and says, "You can't come in." And Joe is telling him, "It's me, Joe Page," and the guy says, "I know, but you can't come in." I guess about this time it must've been about two-thirty or three o'clock in the morning, and we got shut out just like that.

The next afternoon, I'm running in the outfield with Lopat before the game, and he says to me, "What time did you get home last night?'' So I answer, "Oh, I was in bed around eleven," as though I'm a monk or something. But Lopat right away says, "You're a goddamned liar, that's what you are.''

I'm still playing it straight, and I say, like I'm all confused and insulted, "What do you mean, I'm a liar?'' So he tells me, "Well, you know that bar where you and Page were knocking on the window last night around two-thirty or three in the morning? Well, I was inside. I was the guy who told the owner not to let you two characters in. So don't give me that stuff about being in bed by eleven, you bastard, I was there!''

MICKEY:
Page was a big, good-looking guy, and for a while the ball club had a detective trailing him—a lady detective. I don't actually remember anybody following him around after I got with the Yankees, but they told me the front office hired this lady detective to keep an eye on him because he used to run pretty good. I don't think Joe ever got to know who she was, but later they said that it didn't work—she started to fall in love with him at a distance, and that was the end of the stakeout.

Casey was great, though. You couldn't fool him because he'd pulled every stunt that was ever thought up, and he did it fifty years before we even got there. He didn't mind it too much, either, so long as you didn't start to lose it on the ball field. That's where it all came out, on the field. You could run around like some of the guys, or you could travel with the club looking like DiMaggio in those beautiful blue suits and Countess Mara ties. But, either way you did it, if you played like DiMaggio, you'd keep Casey off your back.

WHITEY:
I only knew Casey a little while that first year, but I was getting the idea fast. About three weeks after we won the World

Series against the Phillies, I ran into a friend of mine named Joe Gallagher, out in Astoria where we were living. I said to him, "Joe, I'm going to run up and ask my draft board how many more months I have before I go into the service." I remember the draft board was above the Consolidated Edison office on Broadway and Steinway Street, and we ran upstairs to check it out. And they told me, "You'll be leaving in two weeks."

I was supposed to report on a Monday, I think it was November 19, so on the Friday before, we started a party at my family's apartment in Astoria. Everybody came over—Frank Verdi, who used to play with the Yankees and now was a manager in the farm system, and Tommy Gorman—the pitcher, not the umpire—and some of the guys I played with in the minors, and my girl friend, Joan Foran, and a couple of her girl friends, and some of my father's bartender friends. And the party went on all night. We grabbed an hour's sleep, and then on Saturday some more people would come in and get it started again.

It was one of the funniest things I've ever seen, and now we have half the neighborhood at the house, some asleep, some drinking, the kitchen table is filled with all these bottles of scotch and rye, and there was beer all over the place. Some guy even was sleeping sitting straight up in a chair. We had a ball, all night Saturday and all day Sunday and all night Sunday. Then it's finally Monday morning, time for me to go, and some photographer from the *News* shows up about seven o'clock in the morning and walks into this.

He wants a good-bye picture of my mother making my "last breakfast" for me before I go in the army. So she brings him in the kitchen where we had booze all over the place, and he can't see anything but empty bottles and all the debris from our three days of partying. My mother didn't feel too good as it was, and I felt terrible. But she put a bowl of cereal in front of me after she cleaned off the kitchen table, and we got that little part of the room looking like a typical kitchen again, and she made believe she was serving me a farewell breakfast, all nice and homey. So he took the picture, and they ran it on the back page of the paper, showing "the rookie being served his final breakfast by his mother in Queens." I even had to choke down the bowl of cereal just to get this picture in the *News*.

Hell, the photographer even followed us down to Whitehall Street and took our picture when I was saying good-bye. He still didn't know how our heads were splitting. He thought we were just sad because I was going in and leaving the Yankees and all. But I didn't mind it too much at the time, because I was still single and I wanted to get the two years over with. They sent me to Fort Monmouth over in New Jersey, and that's when I really started missing Joan and Casey and the Yankees.

You know, it was still only a few weeks after the World Series, and I'd only been with the team three or four months and now they're hustling me off to Fort Monmouth. I don't think I even had my check yet for the Series. Besides, after all that, it was tough living on eighty-four dollars a month for two years.

NEW BOYS
ON THE BLOCK

WHITEY:
After three and a half months on the Yankees, I did two years in the Signal Corps and I missed all of the 1951 and 1952 seasons. "Missed" is the right word, too. I was only sixty miles from New York, down at Fort Monmouth, but I was so aggravated because I wasn't able to pitch that I went to very few ball games during that whole time. Maybe three in all, and I didn't go into the locker room once. The next time I saw the guys was the following spring—it was April 14, 1951, and they had just come into New York from Arizona. That was the one year the Yankees trained there, and it was the year Mickey joined the club. We were like the new boys on the old neighborhood block.

I remember the exact date so well because it was the day I got married. I told you I was good at dates.

MICKEY:
I remember it because Casey just got done telling me I'd be staying with the team instead of going back to Joplin or someplace. We went by train from Phoenix to New York by way of California, and I couldn't believe any of it—especially Casey.

You know, he was from California, and once out there he decided to start only guys who came from the state. He had, let's see, Charlie Silvera catching and Tom Morgan pitching, then Fenton Mole at first, Jerry Coleman at second, Gil McDougald was at third and Billy Martin was the shortstop. In the outfield, he put Joe DiMaggio and Jackie Jensen and Gene Woodling. I didn't start that day. I was from Oklahoma.

WHITEY:

By the time the guys got to New York to open the season, Joan and I had the date picked for the wedding. The Yankees usually played the Dodgers three exhibition games just before starting the regular season—this was the year you guys got rained out in Washington and had to open in Yankee Stadium. But that weekend before the club went to Washington, I got a furlough or something and came up to New York and, after the Saturday game with the Dodgers, we took the whole team to the wedding reception in a bus.

Everybody got out to Astoria, where we got married, and they were serving Manhattans before the meal, and I'll never forget Joe and Tommy Henrich coming in and grabbing a few Manhattans. Joan was thrilled they even came. I was impressed they could drink so much.

MICKEY:

I don't remember even meeting Whitey, not even when Skowron and I had that week with the club the September before that. But I do remember I wore Number Six in Ebbets Field that afternoon. And I remember sitting in the back of the bus after the game, going to the wedding and thinking when I got there that I wouldn't mind getting to know Joanie.

WHITEY:

I hadn't gotten to know her myself yet. Anyway, the Yankees asked me to stay over and throw out the first ball when they opened the season the next week. That was okay, even if it was our honeymoon, so I threw out the ball and later, when the game was over, Joan went through the dugout instead of the stands to get out and she fell down the steps and ripped her stockings. We were getting off to a great start.

Finally, we went to Palm Beach for the rest of our honeymoon, and Bruce Henry called me. He was running the West Palm Beach Indians then, and he was the only person who ever gave me a cut in salary. That happened a few years earlier, when I was playing in Butler, Pennsylvania, and making $250 a month. I had about a 13-and-3 record there and was promoted to Norfolk, Virginia, which was in class-B. And the first thing Bruce did—he was running *that* club then—was cut me down to $200 a month.

Now he calls me up on the telephone on my honeymoon and asks me to pitch batting practice for his West Palm Beach Indians. And I'm still in the Army and all I've got is a thirteen-day furlough.

After all that—the drinking at the reception and falling down the steps and pitching batting practice on our honeymoon—it's a wonder Joan stuck it out. But we finally got back up to Fort Monmouth and got an apartment, and it worked okay. I was stationed there for the next two years; I was supposed to be a clerk or something in the Signal Corps, but I was actually made the groundskeeper for the baseball field in the summertime. They did that so I could pitch. Mule Haas, the old outfielder for the Athletics, was our manager—he was a civilian, but he managed the team anyway. And I'll never forget my first summer there in '51. He had me pitching on Tuesday, Thursday, and Saturday, and he even wanted me to pitch on Sunday, which was an off-day when I could go home if I wanted.

Finally I said that I didn't mind pitching two or even three games a week, but four was ridiculous. It was only five or six innings at a time and I could do it physically, but I still wanted to sneak home on Sunday. So one Sunday I didn't show up for a game, and Monday I was told that I had been thrown off the team.

So I joined the Monmouth Beach Tavern Softball Team instead, and played softball with them for the rest of the summer. They were a bunch of guys from a bar on the beach where Joan and I had the apartment. I still don't know whose idea it was to throw me off the army team, but the following year they let me come back and pitch for the summer—but only once or twice a week. Casey would've died if he knew about that four-times-a-week stuff the summer before.

MICKEY:
Casey was dying anyway because he had me playing right field that year; it was '51 and I was a rookie, and I was striking out and getting pissed off all the time. I remember one day I was still standing out in the field thinking about how I just struck out and I didn't get any jump on a fly ball that was hit. And when we came in after the inning, Lopat got me in a corner of the dugout and yelled at me. ''You want to play?'' he said, and I was sort of scared all the time anyway. ''If not, get your ass the hell out of here. We don't need guys like you. We want to win.''

They wanted to win, all right. It was a pretty neat time to win at almost any game or business: World War II was over, people were rushing to reclaim their homes and jobs and pleasures, television and the jet airplane were revolutionizing life (and especially social life), and the inflation of the war economy had made it clear that you probably had to win big in order to pay the bills.

There was plenty of opportunity, though, to cash in. The New York Yankees, for example, didn't need the insights of a mathematical wizard to read the equation: In 1945, the final year of the war, they finished fourth in the American League—their lowest ranking in twenty years—and they did it before 881,846 customers. But the next season, with the pattern of life and leisure fast returning to "normal," they edged their way up to third place—but drew 2,265,512 customers. So that was the start of the joyride; at least, at the turnstiles. For the next four seasons, they played before 2,000,000 or more cash-carrying fans every summer; and for the next fourteen seasons, before 1,400,000 or more. What they needed then was the team to keep the turnstiles clicking, and they imported Stengel on that rainy day in 1948 to marshal the manpower.

The Professor wasted no time providing the appropriate melodrama. His first bunch of Yankees, in 1949, suffered a total of seventy-three injuries—including one that kept Joe DiMaggio out of the ball park for half the season—and entered the final two days of the schedule one game behind the Boston Red Sox, who were led by the former Yankee manager Joe McCarthy. In two tumultuous days in their packed stadium in the Bronx, they somehow survived and snatched the pennant on the last day, then rolled on to win the World Series against the Brooklyn Dodgers in five games.

For an encore, they took the pennant by three games in 1950, then swept Philadelphia in the Series with Ford pitching the final game and Mantle crushing rocks with a sledge-hammer in the zinc mines back in Oklahoma. Then in 1951, they led the pack by five games and beat the "miracle" Giants in six games in the Series, with Ford in the Signal Corps and Mantle in right field. The Giants, who had won the National League pennant on Bobby Thomson's celebrated home run in the ninth inning of the third playoff game against Brooklyn, played the series with a rookie named Willie Mays in center field flanked by Henry Thompson and Monte Irvin—giving them the first black outfield in the major leagues.

In 1952, Ford was playing for the Monmouth Beach Tavern Softball Team and Mantle was in center field because DiMaggio now was retired. They made it four straight pennants, winning by two games, and then four straight World Series, winning in seven over the Dodgers. Finally, in 1953, they won by eight and one-half games, took the World Series in six over the Dodgers and made history as the first team ever to dominate the business five summers in a row. The Series fell a few dollars short of becoming the first $3,000,000 Series on record; the television fees, already becoming a significant part of baseball revenue, totaled $925,000; radio brought in $200,000; a pre-game TV program was worth $100,000; each Dodger got $6,178 for losing; each Yankee, including Stengel, got $8,280 for winning.

WHITEY:

When I finally got out of the army, it was late in 1952 and the Yankees were mailing out their contracts for the next season. I was still broke. I owed my mother-in-law money, I owed my other in-laws money, and I owed my parents money. Don't forget, I was 9 and 1 for those three months I pitched before going in the army. So I told Roy Hamey, who was the general manager then, that I wanted ten thousand dollars for that first year I was out of the service. He offered me seven thousand. I dropped down to nine, and then he went up to eight. I still wasn't ready to take it, but he said: "We'll give you eight thousand, we'll go up to eight, but if you ain't on the next plane to St. Petersburg, I'm dropping it back down to seven thousand again." So I got on the next plane to St. Pete.

I think I roomed with Tommy Gorman or Frank Verdi. It must've been Verdi, because that was his only year with the Yankees. He was a shortstop, which was too bad because so was Rizzuto. Frank got into one game that season, and never even got to bat officially. That was 412 times less than Rizzuto got to bat that season.

I used to room with Billy Martin then at the Soreno, that big old hotel in downtown St. Pete a couple of blocks from the water. I remember it because I came into the room once that spring and caught Billy on a date with a nurse. Don't ask me why I remember things like that. Same reason I remember the first time my wife came to spring training, maybe the year after that, I guess it was '54. Billy was still staying at the Soreno, and Merlyn and I stayed at a place called Morgan's Cottages.

One night I went over to the hotel and picked up Billy, and we went to the dog track. On the way home from the track, we stopped at Chick's Rancho or someplace like that by the track, and there were two girls there, and Billy was dancing with them and wanted to drive them home. So he got in the back with one and I got in the front with the other one. He said, just take me to her house, and so I did. And we even stopped by the ball park where we had spring training. And anyway, it was pretty good and late by the time I got home myself.

The next morning, Ralph Houk and Charlie Silvera stopped by to pick me up and go to the ball park (they were living in Morgan's Cottages, too). So I just jumped up and washed my face and threw on some clothes, and we took off. But when I came home from the ball park that night, there were my clothes stacked up right on the front doorstep, and Merlyn had the car packed and little Mickey in it and everything. And she just left me standing right there, and drove all the way back to Oklahoma by herself.

WHITEY:
People are going to think we didn't do anything in spring training but horse around. But I remember one time in the

spring when we went over to Miami to play the Dodgers in an exhibition game, and some of the guys later rented a fishing boat. Joe Page and George Sternweiss and some other guys. They got Joe Page hooked into the chair, you know, sitting in that chair with the pole attached to it. We didn't catch anything, so we finally told Page he might as well go in and lay down in the boat for a while and take a nap. If he got a bite on his line, we would wake him up.

So sure enough, he went in and fell asleep. Right away they pulled his line in and they got a bucket with a handle on it and they tied the line to it and put it under water so the farther out it went, the harder it got to pull it in. The captain was in on it, so he ran the boat faster, and the faster he'd go the harder this thing would pull on the line.

So they ran in and they woke up Page and yelled that he had a bite on his line. Joe jumped up and hopped into his chair and got all strapped into it again, and he was fighting this thing for maybe an hour or so, back and forth. The captain would slow the boat down and Page would get it in a little bit. Then he'd speed the boat up, and the line'd pull like hell again. And finally after an hour of this, Page was just about finished.

We knew he couldn't last much longer, so the captain slowed the boat down and Joe reeled this thing in about thirty feet or so from the back of the boat. And all he could see then was the top of this pail that he thought was a fish all that time, and he said, "Look at the mouth on that son of a bitch." Finally he yanked it in closer and found out it was only the pail, and he chased Sternweiss around the boat for the rest of the trip back in.

Later we got back to St. Pete after this trip to Miami, and Sternweiss would take an old broom into the locker room and he'd get a pail and a rope and tie the pail to the broom. Then he'd go running around the clubhouse hollering to Page to go bucket-fishing with him, and Page would start chasing him around the clubhouse the way he did on the boat in Miami.

MICKEY:

Casey was smart, because he got onto us right away after we started goofing around and he always pretended like he was mad at us, even if he wasn't. When the club was going bad, he'd have a meeting and tear into the guys, and he'd always point out Whitey and Billy and me in the meetings. Or else he'd say something so the other guys *thought* he was pointing us out. I think he did it to show the older players on the club that we new guys weren't getting away with anything just because we maybe were having a big year on the field. He really liked us, but he'd lay into us at the meetings, and then on the way out he'd throw us that big wink of his.

WHITEY:

The older players started to get on us, too. I mean, it didn't take too long. They'd tell me to quit fooling around. I'll never forget in Chicago once, I thought it was a two o'clock game but it was a one o'clock game, and I was rooming with Yogi at the time. Yogi went down and had breakfast and I said, "Wake me up before you go to the park." But he forgot to call me back, and it was around twelve o'clock by the time I woke up. But I didn't think there was any big sweat because I was still figuring it was a two o'clock game, so I went on down to the dining room in the hotel. When I got there, though, there was nobody else around, and then I started thinking it was sort of strange.

Red Patterson, our publicity man, was the only person sitting there, and he said something like you'd better hurry the hell up, the game starts at one o'clock and you're pitching. And it's like twenty after twelve now. Christ, I jumped into a cab and I got to the park at about twenty minutes to one, and you have to start warming up usually at least fifteen minutes before they start the game. By now, Stengel and Turner are going crazy, they didn't know where the hell I was.

So I rushed inside and changed my clothes and got ready, then I hurried back outside and warmed up for about nine or ten minutes. And that's the time I remember Hank Bauer saying to me, sort of tough, "Don't be fooling with *my* money."

When I finally went out and started pitching, I was nervous as hell and I kept hearing Bauer's voice in my head saying, "Don't be fooling with my money." We won the game something like 10 to 0, but after that I made sure I got to the park on time.

That's the way it was when you tried to "make" a club as established as the Yankees were then. We young guys were more or less afraid of the older guys like the Gene Woodlings and Ralph Houks and Joe DiMaggios. You know, Vic Raschi or Eddie Lopat or Allie Reynolds would say something, and we'd listen. And DiMaggio: Just one stare from him was worth a thousand words.

Some people used to think Frank Crosetti kept us in line. You know, the coach who'd give us sermons about how to act "like a Yankee." But I don't remember that Frank went around giving us any lectures. He used to tell me that he liked my attitude because, if I pitched and won, I'd act the same as if I was knocked out in the second inning. I'd just walk into the dugout and into the dressing room and have a beer.

MICKEY:
Cro used to get pissed off when I'd go in and kick hell out of the water cooler or something like that because I just struck out with a couple of guys on base. The thing that helped, I guess, was that Cro was usually out on the third-base coaching line and didn't see half of what was going on in the dugout.

WHITEY:
The very first day I was with the ball club, Lopat grabbed me and started banging it into my mind that you had to *live* the

game, no matter what you did on your own time. You'd have to know how to pitch to *every* hitter in the league. We'd sit on the bench when neither of us was pitching, and he'd just call the pitches on every hitter who went up to the plate. This guy is a low-ball hitter, this guy is a high-ball hitter, this guy is a bad curve-ball hitter. He'd keep stressing how important it was knowing their weaknesses. And I was the type of pitcher who was a lot like Lopat, maybe a little faster, but I had the same style—I had to rely on control to get them out, the way he did.

When you're a kid, you really think of players as supermen. Then when you get there, you realize what it takes to play ball in the big leagues, and they're *really* supermen. It was DiMaggio's next-to-last year when I got there, and he was thirty-four or thirty-five, but he was really graceful in center field, whatever age he was.

And Yogi was already smart as hell at calling a game, outguessing the hitters, and he'd drive some of them crazy. Ted Williams would come up there trying to bear down the way he did all the time, concentrating for God's sake on just hitting me, and I'd look down and see Yogi squatting behind the plate and throwing some dirt on Williams' shoes. Every once in a while, he'd glance down and realize what was happening and tell Yogi to go screw himself—but by then he was distracted.

Yogi had problems when he was coming up, when he was one of the "new kids." Trouble throwing the ball and things like that. But I think Bill Dickey made a good catcher out of him, the way Turner and Lopat worked with me on my pitching. You'd never think Yogi was fast, but he was quick as hell behind the plate. When they'd hit those little dribblers out in front of the plate, he'd come springing out of there like they shot him out with a rifle.

They paid Yogi ninety dollars a month when he signed back in 1942, I think it was. Later, Casey wouldn't make a move without writing his name down on the lineup card. One season he caught 151 games out of 154. When Allie Reynolds was pitching his no-hitter in 1951—it was his second one; he had pitched one against Cleveland in July and now he was pitching another against Boston late in September—Yogi was his catcher. They got down to two outs in the ninth inning with Ted Williams up, and Yog called for a high fast ball across the letters and tight. Allie gave it to him and Williams hit it a mile high, but foul over toward the dugout, and Yogi goes chasing it and loses it at the last minute and falls down and everything, and Williams gets another swing.

I wasn't there, but Yogi told me later that he just went back and squatted down and signaled for the same pitch all over again. He's got to be the luckiest bastard in the world. Williams was one guy who might've hit it out of sight if you gave him another swing, but Reynolds pitches another fast ball tight across the letters and he hits it in the exact same place as the first one—straight up in the air and foul over by the dugout. But this time, Yogi makes Goddamned sure he squeezes it, and Allie gets his second no-hitter.

CASEY STENGEL:
I thought Reynolds was gonna catch that one himself. I'll tell you where Berra was pretty good as a ball player. People don't understand it. He put time in on the sport; he knew everything about different sports. He'd like to sit and watch. Berra was pretty good, too, watching pitching. He was *very* good when he saw them get careless.

MICKEY:
The year after that, we won the pennant for the fourth straight time and Yogi hit thirty home runs, and I think that was a record for any catcher. We hit 129 as a club, and somebody told me that we set—either set or tied—something like twenty-nine records. It was our first year without DiMaggio, and I set a record, too: I struck out 111 times. But when we got into the World Series with the Dodgers, we did

okay. I remember Duke Snider hit four home runs for them, but Yogi and I got a couple each for Casey, and Johnny Mize got into only like five of the seven games and he hit three out for us. It always seemed like it was that way, when we needed a shot, somebody'd get up and give it. Like Billy. He got something like only three home runs all year, but in the series he hit one out and pestered hell out of the Dodgers in the field.

WHITEY:

After I got back to the club from Monmouth and Roy Hamey told me I better get the next plane to St. Pete, I remember how we opened up that season, 1953, in Washington. The Senators had Chuck Stobbs pitching and Mickey hit one over the bleachers and all the way out of Griffith Stadium. Red Patterson rushed outside the park with a tape measure and hunted around till he found some kid who chased the ball across the street into a yard. So Red paced off the distance back to the wall of the bleachers, he figured out it was 50 feet high at the wall, added something like 69 feet for the bleachers and 391 feet to home plate, and he said the ball went 565 feet from where Mickey hit it.

We won the pennant that year and made it five straight, which nobody ever came close to doing before. Then we played the Dodgers again in the Series and Billy hit about .500; I think it was exactly .500, he got twelve hits, a couple of homers and a couple of triples. Yogi got nine hits, and one of them was a home run, too, and I remember Charlie Dressen took out Johnny Podres after he got the bases loaded by hitting Bauer on the wrist and walking Yogi. He brought in Russ Meyer to pitch to Mickey, and he hit it in the upper deck in left. I remember something else, too. It was my first World Series since I beat the Phillies and went into the army in 1950, and Casey started me in the fourth game. They got three runs off me and I was gone after one inning.

MICKEY:

That was the year we got into trouble with the club by signing the tab at the Latin Quarter.

WHITEY:

That was the year. It was right after we won the pennant for the fifth time, and we went down to the Latin Quarter—me and you and Billy and our wives, and I think Andy Carey and Gus Triandos. A few drinks, and we ordered a couple of bottles and we're celebrating, and now comes the waiter with the bill and it comes to seventy or eighty dollars or something like that.

First Billy wanted to pick it up himself, then we all decide we're going to chip in. But I see Dan Topping at another table with a big group of friends, so I say, Naw, let's sign Topping's name to it. So I take the bill and just sign Topping's name on it—but I also sign Mantle, Ford and Martin on it. I didn't want to get Carey and Triandos in any trouble. We put in a big tip, and maybe the whole thing comes to a hundred dollars.

The next day, we get a call from Hamey or Topping, saying we're fined five hundred dollars each. I couldn't believe it. I kept saying, "Is he kidding? We win the pennant, and he's going to fine us five hundred dollars for a silly thing like that?"

Finally, we win the Series against the Dodgers, and Billy's the hero with his twelve hits and all, and we're having the victory party, the whole club. And Billy and Mickey corner Topping over by the bar, and I see him starting to take out his pen and write out some checks. Then they come over to the table I'm sitting at and say, "Hey, go over to the bar and he'll write you a check for the five hundred dollars."

But you know me. I just say, "Tell him to stick it up his ass." But in the middle of the following summer, he sends me the check, anyway.

We always got along pretty good with Topping. You very seldom saw him or George Weiss or Del Webb during the season. Webb more than anyone, because he lived out on the Coast and when he did come to New York, he always stopped down in the dressing room.

You would see them maybe three or four times the whole year, that's all. They just let Stengel run the club, headaches and all. And Casey ran it pretty good.

ON THE ROAD

$\mathbb{B}$aseball teams travel like the circus: together, town to town, tied tightly to the day's performance. In the 1950s, they still took the train for the short moves down the road, but they also began to buy blocks of space on the new jet airliners that were revolutionizing travel for just about everything *except* the circus.

The working season opened in mid-February when most of the sixteen teams then in the National and American Leagues headed for spring training in the Florida resorts; the rest settled in Arizona. And for six weeks or so, that was the nearest anybody came to leading a "normal" life: six weeks in one place. After that, if you still were on the payroll of the traveling troupe, you spent six months back North playing out the schedule of 154 games from April until October: half of them "at home"—even though your real home might be in Lost Nation, Iowa—and the other half on the rails, on the rush, on the road.

The entourage might number forty or forty-five persons with contrasting specialties and backgrounds: twenty-five professional players, one manager (professional but sometimes transient), four coaches, one trainer, perhaps one public relations man, half a dozen or more newspaper men (known loosely but invariably as "the writers"), two or three broadcasters and one "traveling secretary," who was the ringmaster.

The road secretary also was a little like Noah, herding his species into the ark, booking them into hotels two by two, chartering the "team bus" to collect them at the hotel two and a half hours before the game, and later, an hour after the game, handing out the per diem checks for "meal money," hiring the truck to transport baggage and equipment to airport or depot—and serving as the manager's messenger or even executioner for everything from sending emergency telegrams to policing midnight curfews.

For the New York Yankees, the road secretary also acted as deputy chief of staff to Casey Stengel, who went to his first ball games just after the turn of the century in horse-drawn surreys and who was shepherding his flock aboard Boeing 727 jetliners fifty years later. "I was fairly good at times," he reflected once, referring to his flair for playing the game, not to his flair for skirting the rules. "But a lot of people seem to remember some of the stunts I pulled better than they do the ball games I helped win." Then, pressed for a more precise report on his half-century on the road, he acknowledged: "I was always in a lot of damn trouble."

One of his flock was Jerry Coleman, the "thinking man's baseball player." Born in San Jose, California in 1924; pilot in the Marine Corps in World War II and again in 1952 and 1953 during the Korean war; pivot man on the double play during Stengel's record run of five straight world championships; a straight arrow with a career batting average of .267 and, in 1955, a broken collarbone; later, a broadcaster for the Yankees and San Diego Padres.

JERRY COLEMAN:
I got there at the end of 1948, so I started with Casey in 1949 at the beginning of the team's heyday—though we didn't realize it at the time. Whitey got there in 1950, but not really till 1953 after he got out of the Army. Mickey showed up in

'51. And, once Joe DiMaggio retired, they became the Yankees. They were the heart and soul of the club not long after they arrived.

Whitey was the oldest young player I ever saw. Nothing seemed to bother him in a game. If you blew a play, he'd say: "Give me the goddamned ball and we'll get them." In the 1957 World Series, I blew the game for him, the fifth game, and maybe the Series.

There was no score in the sixth inning with Eddie Mathews up, and I was playing second base almost back in right field on him. But he hit a slow bouncing ball, and I came running in, thinking, I can either play it safe for a good bounce or charge it hard and take my chances. So I played it safe, and it was the only time I ever heard another player's voice above the crowd: "J-E-R-R-Y-Y-Y!"

It was Whitey covering first base. I don't know where Harry Simpson was, but he wasn't a first baseman anyway. I finally got to the ball and threw it hard to Whitey, but we just missed getting Mathews by that much. Then Henry Aaron dropped a single in front of Mantle and Joe Adcock singled, and they got a run and beat us, 1 to 0. But Whitey never said a thing to me, except when he shouted "J-E-R-R-Y-Y-Y!"

Before that, I roomed with Mickey two years when Billy Martin was in the service, in 1954 and 1955. Look, Joe DiMaggio was the perfect player—on the field and off the field. Mickey was sometimes like a child off the field. He'd sit in the front row of a nightclub and take the spotlight and all, but he never had a vicious thing on his mind, and as a roommate he was the most considerate person in the world. He was like a mouse. Some guys were always snapping on the light or flushing the john when you were sleeping, but not him.

In St. Pete, we had houses a couple of blocks apart during spring training and we had a car pool. He was supposed to pick me up at nine-fifteen in the morning to go to the field. I'd look out and he'd already be parked outside. Maybe he got there early, but he didn't honk the horn or get impatient or anything. He'd say, "I got here ahead of time," sort of apologizing, and I'd think, Here's the best ball player in the American League waiting on me.

But on the field, he had this great drive, competitiveness. He was fierce. He was like two different people. In our room, sometimes he'd be bugged for a while because Yogi was making more money than he was, and he'd say: "I'm leading the league in home runs and everything, why's he making fifty thousand and me only thirty-five?" Like it was a mystery that he couldn't understand. I'd tell him that in baseball, you get paid after the fact—but someday they'll be paying you *more* than you're worth.

Well, okay. He was good and considerate and all. But he wasn't exactly a plaster saint. I guess maybe he took five years off my career.

WHITEY:
Everybody who roomed with Mickey said he took five years off their career.

MICKEY:
Thank you. Actually, first of all, I was Billy's roommate. You know, we lived together in New York City, aside from being roommates on the road, and Whitey was rooming with somebody else then. But we always seemed to get together after the game.

I always heard about Whitey from guys on the team, the ones who knew him before he left for the Army. I was expecting him to be real cocky, kind of smart-aleck. Well, he *was* real cocky, very confident of himself, which is probably why he was such a great pitcher. I think probably he was the best I ever played behind: He got the game over fast. I remember one time we had a team called "Mickey Mantle's All-Stars" that played "Willie Mays' All-Stars" in some exhibition game up in Syracuse, and Johnny Podres pitched for the Willie Mays team and Whitey for us. We beat them, 1 to 0, and I think I hit a home run off of Podres, and the whole game lasted only like an hour and twenty minutes. A real fast game.

And that's the reason I don't think I've ever seen anybody, or ever knew anybody, who didn't really enjoy playing behind Whitey. Everybody will tell you they wanted to play behind him because he got the ball over; he hardly walked anybody ever and he had so much confidence on the mound that it seemed that it dwindled through the rest of the team when he was pitching. I know I had it. I felt like we were never going to get beat when he pitched. And I've always heard about other guys talking about how cocky he was.

Anyway, I thought he was going to turn out kind of like a smart aleck, but instead it turned out that he was probably the nicest guy I ever met in my life. Sure, he had that cocky arrogance on the mound when he was pitching, but when he's off the field, I don't ever remember Whitey getting into an argument with anybody. Whereas Billy—if somebody would say something in a bar, Billy would have to know why and what they said it for, and it would get into an argument. But after Billy got traded, well, it was mostly me and Whitey from that time on. We didn't have very many people running around with us. We'd run into guys, you know, in bars; it wasn't like we were too good for them, in fact it was the other way around. We'd invite them or want to be around other guys, but it'd always seem like we'd wind up alone together.

WHITEY:
Alone together—it sounds like a song title or something. But you get to know guys, rooming with them on the road; you're spending half your life with them.

Like Tommy Gorman, who was my roommate in the minor leagues. He was my roommate at Binghamton, at Kansas City, and then when I went in the Army in '51, he came up and was with the Yankees for a few years. We have been very close over the years, and in fact he is my son Eddie's godfather. Tommy was quite a real straightforward guy, a churchgoing man. But he used to have a weight problem when he was with the Yankees, and Jim Turner was always checking the weight charts when he was the pitching coach to make sure Tommy wasn't getting too heavy.

I used to get a kick out of him when we were on the road and Tom'd be going on a diet. We'd get to the hotel and he'd order cereal with cream and strawberries, then he'd have a couple of eggs with corned beef hash and a big glass of orange juice, a couple of glasses of milk, you know. Finally he'd tell the waitress to bring him whole wheat toast with no butter on it—after he'd knocked off about three thousand calories.

MICKEY:
It was the other way around when I first met Whitey; the thing that surprised me was how small he was. You know, I was always hearing about this "little Whitey Ford," but I didn't exactly believe it. Yet, when he was playing, I think he only weighed 170 or 175, and that surprised me a lot.

I guess before Billy left, he and Whitey and me ran around a lot together. But when Billy got traded, me and Whitey made a deal with the Yankees. By that time we were making pretty good money and the income tax was getting a little heavy, so we made this deal where we'd get our expenses cashed with the club. Also, that we'd have adjoining rooms in the hotels. They'd let us be roommates with separate rooms, and we'd open the adjoining door and turn them into a kind of suite.

I don't know exactly what the deal was, but we had so much money we could spend in the hotel in a year. I don't think we ever reached that plateau, but it was there and it was a good deal if we wanted it. It was very nice of them to do it that way, and I think that was one of the reasons they never had any trouble signing Whitey or me. You know, the Yankees were always so good to both of us that it just would've been silly for us to hold out for more money.

I was making almost the maximum at that time—it's nothing these days, but at that time it was quite a bit of money—and Whitey was making good money, too. So the thing that we wanted was what they let us have: adjoining rooms on the road, expenses we could sign for, things like that.

The way we worked it out was like I'd sign room service for both of us. I'd get up before Whitey and order breakfast from room service, and sign the check. Then he'd do it for dinner, or something like that. We were just like—like, I'll give you an instance. Like we'd have a night game, say, and the next day would be a night game. I'd always wake up like at eight o'clock in the morning and he didn't get up till eleven. So I'd order up a cup of coffee or something and a newspaper, and watch TV, and be real quiet till he woke up at eleven o'clock. And when I thought it was near the time for him to get up, why, I'd order breakfast and a paper for him. We'd eat breakfast and sit around and watch TV for a couple of hours, or go to a movie, something like that, and that would be our day. Maybe at five o'clock it'd be time to get on the bus and go to the ball game.

Well, then after the game, most of the time we'd go out and have a few drinks and a dinner.

What I really liked about Whitey, and what he liked about me, was we didn't talk baseball very much. You know, we'd watch the TV and it wasn't one of those deals where he'd say to me, "Geez, you should have caught the ball last night." Or, if he had a bad day, I never said anything about his day, you know. We just seemed to work out good.

It bugged me more than it did him—the games did. If I had a bad day, it really stayed on my mind, because I had to play again the next day. Of course, I imagine it would be really tough on a pitcher, and this is where his confidence came out. He could have a really terrible day—he didn't have many of them, but he could have one—and he wouldn't let it get him down. And remember, he wouldn't get a chance at it again for four more days.

I don't think I ever remember him worrying about his game. I mean, he always knew he was going to come back out and win the next game. Or that he'd pitch a good game, whether we were going to win it or not. He usually pitched a pretty good game, anyway. Whereas, if I went into a slump, maybe like 0 for 15, I imagine it got pretty quiet in the room. I'd worry about it a lot more, it seemed, than he did. And he was good to be around when you were going bad.

I guess my biggest fault in baseball was striking out too much, and that was because when I hit left-handed, I'd uppercut a little bit and swing too hard at the ball. He used to tell me, like just before we'd walk out of the room, he'd say, "Come on now, let's see a short, choppy stroke today." Like he was telling me I was swinging too hard. He wouldn't go into it too much, just, "Let me see that short choppy stroke."

He wasn't tense before he pitched, but he was maybe different then. He'd never go out the night before he pitched. Well, maybe once in a while he did, but not very often. Most of the time, if he was pitching the next day, he'd even leave the game a little early and go home and go to bed. I wouldn't bother him then. If he hadn't gone to bed when I got home, we might watch the late-night movie on TV or something. I didn't ever ask him to go out with me those nights, I just figured he didn't want to. Some nights like that, I'd go out with some of the other guys.

But when Whitey pitched, he always felt like unwinding that night after the ball game. And that's when most of our breaking would come on. I always felt good, too, especially if he won the game. I always liked to win, too; I couldn't stand to lose. But if he pitched a good game, I was always ready to celebrate it with him. Lucky for both of us, he won like 236 games when he was pitching for the Yankees.

WHITEY:

When Mickey uses a word like "celebrate," everybody will think of one thing, so we might as well make it a real good confession. We started off drinking beer when we got with the club, then later on we went to scotch with lemon peel, and then Jack Daniel's with orange juice. That's right, Jack Daniel's with orange juice.

When we started to fly on trips, I didn't like the idea so much, and I'd always have to take a few drinks before I got on the plane. It made me feel good; it was as simple as that. Mickey and I would play cards or something and, on takeoff, I used to hold onto that curtain on the window and Mickey would say: "Don't pull that thing off." I'd be squeezing it so tight.

Mickey wasn't as skittish about flying as I was. When we first started flying, I didn't care for it at all, but now I don't mind. In those earlier days, though, if we got to the airport and had a half-hour to kill, I would have a couple of Jack Daniel's to calm me down before the flight. Yeah, with orange juice.

I mentioned scotch with lemon peel. We used to like drinking that at one stage of things, and that's how we "caught" Billy one night at a place called the Ringside Ranch in Chicago. We were drinking there—it's a hillbilly place—and Billy was drinking real slow. We'd order a round, and so on, and finally Billy had four or five lined up in front of him. We were drinking ours at about the same pace—the same for us, but a lot faster than Martin—and Mickey and I went over to put some money in the jukebox. When we came back and looked at Billy, his five glasses all were empty. Just like that, and he said he'd chug-a-lugged them down. We looked in the glasses, but there wasn't any ice. No lemon peels, either.

I'll be a son of a bitch if he could've swallowed all five drinks down so fast, but he was standing there all prim and proper and not batting an eye, as if he did it that way all the time, anyway. But right next to the bar there was this little radiator, and they had one of those fire buckets filled with water. And Mickey happened to look in there, and floating on top was some ice—and five lemon peels. That's how far you could trust Billy when he was trying to get the edge.

MICKEY:

I guess the last time we ever had drinks on an airplane, a team airplane anyway, was the time Ryne Duren and Johnny Blanchard had one too many. Ralph Houk was the manager by then, and he was very lenient with us, you know, he treated us without a lot of chicken shit. I always thought he was a great handler of ball players, I always thought what he did was just right, even this time when he finally had enough of the horsing around.

This time, I don't know if we'd just won the pennant or what, but it seemed like everybody had quite a bit to drink on the plane. Johnny Blanchard had quite a bit, and he even owned his own liquor store back in Minneapolis for a while. And I guess everybody read about Ryne, how he used to drink. He doesn't drink any more; in fact, he works with little kids around Milwaukee and he really hasn't had a drink for years now. He's real straight and everything now. Anyway, on this airplane this time, everybody was feeling pretty good.

Blanchard was still drinking a lot and feeling pretty good, and he was walking up the aisle of the plane while everybody else was having sort of a ball in their seats or sitting on the arm rests of their seats, the way ball players do on long flights. One of the writers with us was Joe King, who worked for one of those newspapers in New York that later went out of business, the *World-Telegram* it was. He had a red moustache, all neat and trimmed all the time, and he was sitting there asleep when Blanchard came rolling by.

So Johnny just reached over and grabbed ahold of Joe's moustache and jerked out a handful of it. No kidding, he just pulled out a whole bunch of the red moustache. That made King pretty mad, and he went and told Houk about it. Meanwhile we were all sitting in the back of the plane drinking and playing cards when Duren came back and started acting like he was going to throw open the back door. Well, naturally everybody got out of their seats and ran like hell out of there.

But just then, Ralph Houk came down the aisle trying to get Joe King out of his mad, and he walks right into this commotion with Duren pretending he was trying to open the door in the back. You know, we were flying at maybe thirty-five thousand feet at the time. Anyway, between the two of them incidents, that was the last time the Yankees were allowed to order drinks on an airplane. Joe King's moustache and Ryne Duren's back door.

WHITEY:

Ryne was one of those guys we got in trades during the fifties, and he could throw a ball through a wall. I think he started with Baltimore in 1954, the first year after they moved from St. Louis. We got him from Kansas City and he pitched for the Yankees about four years till they traded him to the Los Angeles Angels.

He was like Reynolds and Early Wynn and all those guys who never let you forget that they had smoke and weren't afraid to pour it on. Also, everybody read about how Ryne used to drink, so the hitters were never too sure of his condition when he came into a game. And he wore these big, thick, bottle-top eyeglasses and peered through them like he couldn't see anything: home plate or the batter or even the backstop. Then he'd start warming up on the mound and fire the first one over everybody's head—the catcher and umpire and all—right back to the screen. He wanted you to think he was that wild so you wouldn't dig in too much on him. And maybe he was, at that.

MICKEY:

Hell, we spent a lot of time pulling stunts. Like when Cletis Boyer was with the club, and he was one of the biggest practical jokers we had, he'd do almost anything for a laugh. I remember once he came home late one night and he had this girl with him, so he telephoned one of the other players and asked him if he'd like this girl to come up to his room for a little visit.

The guy said, why sure, you know, and he asked Cletis what she looked like and everything, and Boyer said she was pretty and she'd always followed the guy's career playing ball and admired him and all that. She'd just like very much to come up to his room.

So the guy said send her up, and he started to get all dressed for this date and all. Then Cletis would call up another ball player and this time the girl would get on the phone. Of course, the guy never heard Cletis talking, only the girl, and the girl asked this guy—you know, told him the same story, that she'd always admired him and that she had a room in the hotel and why didn't he come down.

Now the second player gets up out of bed and takes a shower and gets dressed up, and it's two o'clock in the morning anyway, so he has to get all dressed and everything. Then he goes down and knocks on the door where the girl is supposed to be staying. Only he's knocking on the door of the other *guy* instead, so they'd both wind up at the door at two in the morning.

WHITEY:

When I got back to the club from the army back in '53, I remember one thing that happened on the road that nearly ended all those little stunts. There was a bunch of us that all piled in a car in St. Louis one night, Tommy Gorman and I and Mickey and Billy and Gene Woodling, Charlie Silvera, Bill Miller and Houk. We went over to East St. Louis, where there was always a lot going on.

We decided to go to some club there, where Ben Blue was playing. He had some girls in his show and he would invite people up from the audience onto the stage. Well, Tommy Gorman and I were watching the show and the rest of the guys were out at the bar in the back. Ben Blue started calling people up, and Tommy and I had to go up and dance the polka or something. Us and other people from the audience would get up and dance as part of the act.

But during the act, we began to hear this commotion out at the bar. The show was just about over anyway, so we went hustling back and got there just when it looked like a big brawl was going to break out. Billy had gotten into an argument with the bartender, as usual, and Houk got involved in it, as usual. Silvera and Houk and Woodling are now agitating, and the next thing I know, this little guy who says he's the owner of the place comes up to Houk with a revolver in his hand. And Ralph looks at him and is ready to pick up a bottle or something, saying something like "that don't scare me."

So Ralph reaches for a bottle, and this little guy turns around and runs back into his office with the gun still in his hand and Houk is saying, "That don't scare me." I guess it didn't, but it sure as hell scared *me*.

We kid a lot now about how much we were fined for some of our tricks. Maybe about a dozen times over the years, but we got most of it back, I guess.

Sometimes Mickey and I would get fined together, sometimes we'd get it separately. But after we were traveling together, they started to think of us as an entry, as though we were a pair of race horses running for the same stable. Casey didn't seem to get too uptight about us, but one time we sort of thought the traveling secretary might be nervous about it— like going back to George Weiss with stories about us. So that time we got together and planned something just for him, on the team bus in Chicago.

Mickey and I got back after a Saturday game and went to the Del Prado Hotel, where we were all staying, and we caught the end of the golf tournament on TV and then ordered room service for our dinner. We sat around all evening watching TV and were in bed by ten-thirty or eleven o'clock. That's what the man said: ten-thirty or eleven o'clock.

The next morning, we got on the bus to go to the park to play the White Sox and we sat right in back of the traveling secretary. Then I said to Mickey, "Gee, how are you going to play today after getting in at six in the morning?" And Mickey said, "How the hell are you going to pitch, you were with me?"

Sure enough, after the road trip, Weiss called us into his office in New York and we were fined $250 each for being late in Chicago. And that was after never leaving our room.

We got it back, though, after we told him what happened. I guess we were damned if we did and damned if we didn't. Maybe that's why Bauer would get hold of a guy and tell him, "Don't be fooling around with *my* money." He didn't always know if you were really fooling around, he just wasn't taking any chances.

MICKEY:
Neither was Casey. Whenever he'd give us one of those clubhouse sermons about staying out late and doing a lot of drinking, he'd finish up by saying, "And some of you milkshake drinkers ain't doin' so hot, either."

Maybe he didn't know where we were the night before, but he wasn't taking any chances, either. After all those years of traveling around himself, I guess he knew that nothing can screw up a ball player like too many rich, heavy, thick milkshakes.

City boy: Street-smart, but "too small" for professional baseball, Eddie Ford starts wearing out the sandlots of New York as a teen-ager with the Thirty-fourth Avenue Boys. He pitches, plays first base, even helps hold the pennant: front row, behind the "K" in Kiwanis.

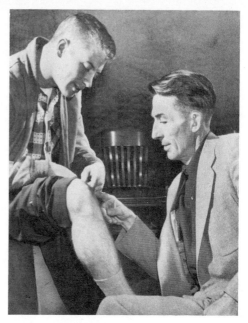

Country boy: Dirt-poor, wearing the homemade uniform of the Baxter Springs Whiz Kids in rural Oklahoma, the switch-hitting son of a miner, Mickey Charles Mantle starts *his* travels with two constants —damaged knees and Tom Greenwade, a scout for the New York Yankees.

Their orbits cross in 1950. But after three months with the "big team," Ford takes a two-year detour into the army. He emerges occasionally to exercise his left arm for Steve O'Neill of the Boston Red Sox and Casey Stengel of the Yankees . . .

. . . who already are fortified with the right arm of Allie Reynolds (two no-hitters in 1951), the left arm of Eddie Lopat and the bankroll of Del Webb.

The city slicker spent some of his $7,000 bonus on a record-player for his parents. The country boy gets $1,500 and pretty soon has wheels and a license plate crammed with the magic number "7," courtesy of the state of Oklahoma. (*Associated Press.*)

His first home in the big city is an apartment shared with Hank Bauer and Johnny Hopp. They live over the Stage Delicatessen in Manhattan. Result: Mantle gains some savoir-faire and twenty pounds.
(*Ernest Sisto*, The New York Times.)

The master of the Yankees, Charles Dillon Stengel, turns out in striped pants, shined shoes and windbreaker as he surveys an empire that is en route to ten pennants in twelve summers.

Man with two prodigies: a pitcher who follows his admonition that "it takes 27 outs to win". . .

. . . and a power hitter who wins the Triple Crown in 1956 and tries it on for size. (*Both photos by Ernest Sisto,* The New York Times.)

They are the Yankees of Joe
DiMaggio, too. How do the two
new prodigies react when they
first meet their hero? Speech-
less. But between them, Joe
and Mickey patrol center field
for the Yankees for nearly thirty
summers.
Ernest Sisto, The New York
Times.

There's nothing wrong with covering center field like this. Jim Rivera of the Chicago White Sox, the guy who hit the ball, and Hank Bauer, the right fielder, both agree . . .

. . . and Larry Doby of the White Sox, who hit this one, also agrees. On good knees or bad, it's like covering everything hit into Death Valley. (*Both photos by Ernest Sisto,* The New York Times.)

But basically, Mantle provides the power at bat that has been the Yankees' trademark since Babe Ruth, and Denny McLain of the Detroit Tigers knows it. (*Ernest Sisto*, The New York Times.)

Sometimes he swings so hard his knees buckle. . .

. . . and sometimes, after popping up in the All-Star Game, he swings even harder afterwards to release his frustration.

When he hits the five hundredth home run of his Yankee career, Mickey gets the glad hand from the senior Yankee of them all, Frank Crosetti. As a third-base coach, "Cro" saw a lot of home runs but rarely extended the traditional handshake. He makes an exception on this one . . .

. . . Everybody's getting in the act. That's Brother Fo rounding the bag to Crosett applause as he hits No. 3 in h career, putting him 497 behir Mick.
(*Both photos by Ernest Sis* The New York Times.)

But for 498 games in regular
seasons, 22 in the World Series
and 12 in All-Star appearances,
Slick earns his nickname as the
ranking left-hander in town . . .

. . . and, in the catcher's-eye
view, he is clearly the Chairman
of the Board of the dynasty in
the Bronx.

Backstage, in the carpeted clubhouse, the dynasty signs dozens of baseballs and shows the smiles of success: Mantle with Elston Howard, the first and foremost black star to make the team.
(*Ernest Sisto,* The New York Times.)

They are also the Yankees of Yogi Berra, who got 2,150 hits in his career, and who welcomes Mantle as The Switcher passes 2,001.
(*Larry Morris,* The New York Times.)

And they are the Yankees of Roger Maris, who teams with Mantle in 1961 for the heaviest home-run barrage in history: 115 between them.

And they are the Yankees of Ralph Houk, the catcher who becomes manager, general manager and then manager again. Mantle remembers, "Then Ralph Houk came along and changed my whole idea of thinking about myself. He told me, 'You are going to be my leader. You're the best we've got.' "

But day in and day out,
for a generation,
they are the Yankees
of Mick and Slick.

INSIDE
THE YANKEE YARD

"I was there the day it opened," James A. Farley was saying, "I don't remember much about the game, but I was there—and have been, for many years since. I used to sit on the third-base side but switched to first base later. Maybe it was when the Yankees switched dugouts, and I wanted to be on the home-team side.

"Why did Yankee Stadium become the showplace?" He peered through the years, back through the seventies, the sixties, through World War II, the Great Depression, the four elections of the man he had called "Boss," back to the days when he was the Democratic Chairman of Rockland County, New York, and a pretty good first baseman himself. Back to the day, April 18, 1923, when they had played the first ball game in Yankee Stadium.

"It was partly the city," he said, answering his own question. "New York's the place. Partly the team that played there: the Yankees. Mostly, it was Babe Ruth. He came in during John McGraw's heyday with the Giants and took over."

Before they opened the doors, before Babe Ruth "took

over," New York belonged to John Joseph McGraw, a graduate of the old Iron and Oil Baseball League of the 1880s and of the tough old Baltimore Orioles of the 1890s. He was five and a half feet tall with straight hair parted left of center above a square face and an immovable look. And when he arrived in 1902 as the manager of the Giants, he wore high starched collars, four-in-hand ties, a fleur-de-lis pin embedded grandly in the center and, against the cold of New York's winter, a fur-collared greatcoat and beaver hat. "His very walk across the field in a hostile town," observed Grantland Rice, "was a challenge to the multitude."

For the next generation, McGraw's very walk across the field indeed became a challenge to the multitude except on the island of Manhattan, where he dominated the sporting and theatrical life of the big city. His team barreled its way to the top while Ethel Barrymore kept neat scorecards from the box seats, Al Jolson raised his arms over his head to acknowledge the cheers, George M. Cohan and Eddie Foy, Jr. waved to the crowds, and DeWolf Hopper lingered between recitations of "Casey at the Bat." Whoever they were, whatever stage they might perform on by night, they gravitated to McGraw's stage uptown by day and watched his Giants— Christy Mathewson, Rube Marquard, Josh Devore, Fred Snodgrass, Chief Meyers, and even Jim Thorpe.

They drummed their fingers to tunes like "Slide, Kelly, Slide," and "Our National Game," which adorned song sheets with intricate line drawings and crossed American flags, and they watched McGraw bully his team through a remarkable run of success. When he arrived, they had stood eighth and last in the National League; but for the next twelve years, they stood either first or second every summer except for 1907 and 1909. Then for nine more summers starting in World War I, they stood either first or second again.

So they were not challenged, for the public's passion or the public's purse, by any other show in town. Not by the Brooklyn Dodgers across the East River, one of the more remarkable troupes in Western Civilization: a ball team known variously as the Trolley Dodgers, the Robins, and the Bridegrooms; a team whose owner would occasionally wander into barrooms to survey the local clientele on the afternoon's pitching selection; and a team whose right fielder, Charles Dillon Stengel, once doffed his cap and "gave the bird" to the umpire.

Nor were they challenged by the Yankees, one of the eight teams in the new American League, a team that operated from a field at 168th Street and Broadway and that was known as the Highlanders. For a while they were under the guidance of Frank Farrell, a onetime bartender and saloon-keeper who had graduated to more exalted things like running a gambling house and racing stable. His partner was William S. Devery, whose nickname in an era of nicknames was "Big Bill" and whose earlier titles also included bartender as well as prize fighter and policeman.

The Yankees played baseball without distinction until 1915, when they were bought for $460,000 by a pair of well-heeled colonels, Jacob Ruppert and the spectacularly named Tillinghast l'Hommedieu Huston, who were friends of Mc-Graw's and admirers of his Giants. They shared an abiding ambition—to own a ball club—and even tried to buy the Giants until McGraw turned them aside with the friendly suggestion, "How about the Yankees?"

So they anted up for the Yankees, who had just spent four seasons finishing sixth, eighth, seventh, and sixth in an eight-team league. The team promptly rose all the way to fifth, then to fourth and third, but stayed stalled there until 1920—when the colonels anted up $450,000 in cash and loans to the hard-pressed owner of the Boston Red Sox, Harry Frazee, and became the sole possessors of George Herman Ruth. As a rookie fresh out of St. Mary's Industrial School in Baltimore half a dozen years before, he had been known as "Jack Dunn's baby," and by the time he reached New York he had established himself as "Babe" Ruth, the best left-handed pitcher in the American League and the best left-handed hitter anywhere.

With Ruth as their leader, the Yankees immediately began to crowd McGraw in his own backyard, the Polo Grounds, where they had been playing as tenants of the Giants because they had outgrown their own Hilltop Park. The dual occupancy didn't trouble McGraw until Ruth hit town and started to hit home runs at a record rate: fifty-four his first year and fifty-nine the next, while Yankee attendance doubled to 1,289,422. Not only that, but they also started winning pennants, and that was the last straw to McGraw, who finally fumed: "The Yankees will have to build a park in Queens or some other out-of-the-way place. Let them go away and wither on the vine."

Instead, the Yankees migrated to the Bronx, where they built a gleaming new stadium with 950,000 board feet of Pacific Coast fir (shipped through the Panama Canal) for the bleachers; 20,000 cubic yards of concrete, and 2,200 tons of structural steel. When they opened the gates that Wednesday afternoon in 1923, Macy's was offering topcoats for $27.50 to $54.75 because "it is apt to be a bit chilly during the opening game of the baseball season," with caps going for $1.88, Lansdowne hats for $4.89, Tampa blunt cigars for $2.49 per can of fifty, and Three Castles cigarettes for $1.88 "in airtight tins of fifty each."

Inside the park, the festivities were presided over by the High Commissioner of Baseball, the former federal judge named Kenesaw Mountain Landis, who had arrived in what the newspapers decided was "democratic style." He took the Interborough subway. Governor Alfred E. Smith and his wife joined Landis in his private box while John Philip Sousa took the baton in hand and led the Seventh Regiment Band to the center-field flagpole with both the Yankees and Boston Red Sox in the line of march and 74,200 fans, "the greatest crowd in baseball history," settled in the new maple seats. Finally, Babe Ruth hit a three-run home run, the Yankees beat the Red Sox by 4 to 1, and the Battle of Broadway began to slip forever away from John Joseph McGraw.

The battle was fully joined later that year when the Yankees played the Giants in the world series, which opened October 10 in their new stadium. They already had played the Giants in the series the two previous years but both times were beaten back. Now, though, the balance of power was about to shift. The Yankees took them, four games to one, with Ruth hitting three home runs and old Casey Stengel replying with two for the Giants. *Old* Casey Stengel? Well, thirty-three years old, and bow-legged besides. It was twenty-six years before he would return to the stadium as manager of the Yankees, but now he was firing a parting shot for McGraw as one era ended and another began.

Batting left-handed, as usual, in the ninth inning of the first game of the series, he hit a line drive off Joe Bush of the Yankees that to most people looked like a single. But the ball flew over the head of the shortstop, Everett Scott, and bounced between the left fielder, Bob Meusel, and the center fielder, Whitey Witt. And it kept bouncing, too, all the way to the farthest fence, 450 feet away, while Casey kept churning his way around the bases. Rounding second, he was heard to mutter, "Go, legs, go." Rounding third, he half-lost a shoe. Heading home, he started to stagger as Meusel fired a long throw to Scott and Scott fired it home to Wally Schang, the catcher, while Casey slid across the plate and, in the press box, Damon Runyon later sat at his typewriter and put it this way:

> This is the way old Casey Stengel ran yesterday afternoon running his home run home.
> This is the way old Casey Stengel ran running his home run home to a Giant victory by a score of 5 to 4 in the first game of the World Series of 1923.
> This is the way old Casey Stengel ran running his home run home when two were out in the ninth in-

ning and the score was tied, and the ball still bounding around inside the Yankee yard.

This is the way—

His mouth wide open.

His warped old legs bending beneath him at every stride.

His arms flying back and forth like those of a man swimming with a crawl stroke.

His flanks heaving, his breath whistling, his head far back. Yankee infielders, passed by Old Casey Stengel as he was running his home run home, say Casey was muttering to himself, adjuring himself to greater speed as a jockey mutters to his horse in a race, saying, "Go on, Casey, go on."

The warped old legs, twisted and bent by many a year of baseball campaigning, just barely held out under Casey until he reached the plate, running his home run home.

Then they collapsed.

WHITEY:

He was a rare bird, all right. I remember once Bob Kuzava lost a game in the ninth inning when some guy got a hit off him, and the next day he was sitting on the bench not too far from the Old Man. They were the only ones there, because it was before the game, and Kuzava was kind of trying to fade into the woodwork or something; he was still embarrassed about the day before. Finally, Casey says, "What did you throw that fella?" So Bob says, "A curve ball." "Where did it break?" Casey wants to know. And Kuzava says, "Right across here," motioning across his waist, you know. Then Casey says, "If it breaks over the plate, it ain't a curve."

He knew that a curve ball's supposed to be sort of an optical illusion to the hitter and, if it breaks right over the plate, half the illusion's gone. But hell, I guess Casey learned that in 1910 when he played with Kankakee or wherever. He knew people, too—like a Goddamned psychologist. You know, he'd make Yogi catch every game almost and finally Yogi'd try to skip one.

He'd go to Casey and say, "I ain't feeling so good today." And the Old Man would say, "Neither am I. It must be the New York climate."

Casey always said the reason we had such good pitching was because Yogi did the catching. He liked the way he'd handle us pitchers. He'd say: "He may not be built like a ball player, but that's nothing. When I was with the Dodgers, Uncle Robbie used to say that about me, too."

The guys used to kid Yogi about everything—the way he looked, the way he'd swing at bad pitches and knock hell out of them, the way he'd save his money. They said he still had the first buck he ever made, and he made plenty. Mickey and I would fall for a lot of phoney investments, but Yogi always seemed to turn everything into gold. We were still kidding him about how dumb he was, but he already was Vice-President of Yoo-Hoo, the chocolate-drink company. And he'd make us pay for it in the clubhouse, that's how dumb he was.

Casey said once, "They say he's funny. Well, he has a lovely wife and family, a beautiful home, money in the bank, and he plays golf with millionaires. What's funny about that? Money is the last thing Yogi thinks about at night before he goes to sleep."

In spring training one time, after we started to train in Fort Lauderdale, we guys went over to some big hotel in Miami Beach. There was me and Joan, and Mickey and Merlyn, and Yogi and Carmen. We went to a place where they had this room downstairs called Harry's something-or-other, and Don Rickles was appearing there. When he spotted us during his act, he started to get on Mickey pretty bad. He got on us about drinking scotch, me and Mickey, while Roger Maris was home taking sauna baths, drinking milkshakes and exercising, and hitting all those home runs.

Then he turned toward Yogi and said, "No kidding, Yog, what was it—a head-on collision?" It was a funny line, but Carmen hated to hear people take shots at the way he looked and she got teed off and wanted to get up and leave.

Casey had it right, though. He'd say, "Yogi's a peculiar fellow, but he has amazing ability." Whenever the guys would tease him about reading those comic books, Yogi'd say something like, "Yeah, but I notice that whenever I put them down, there's always some guys around ready to pick them up." And I remember once he went to see the movie "Dr. Zhivago," and when he came back to the hotel, somebody asked him what he thought about it, you know, it was such a big saga and all that. And Yogi thought about it for a minute and said, "It sure was cold in Russia in those days."

Some catchers may have had better years than Yogi had in 1955, but not many. I think he played in 147 games—he only missed 7 all season—and he hit 27 home runs and batted in 108 runs. Then in the World Series, he got 10 hits and batted around .410. But it was the first Series we ever lost under Casey, and I'll never forget it. We had won 5 straight and then lost the pennant in '54 to Cleveland, even though we won 103 games. Then the next year we won the pennant again, but lost the Series to the Dodgers.

They had a real good team. Don Newcombe was back from the army and had won twenty games. Duke Snider and Roy Campanella and Carl Furillo all hit over .300, and Gil Hodges wasn't much off it, and Snider hit like forty-two home runs, I think. Some of our guys were hurt, too. Mickey tore a muscle in his thigh and all he could do was pinch-hit the last couple of weeks of the season, and Hank Bauer had a charley horse, and Moose Skowron broke his toe.

In the first game, Furillo hit a home run off me and Snider hit another. But Ellie Howard hit one for us, and it was his first time up in a World Series. Then we were tied, 3 to 3, and Joe Collins got two homers off Newk and we won the game. I'll never forget it, though, because Jackie Robinson stole home on me in the eighth inning and made it 6 to 5. I saw him going in, so I threw a fast ball right over the plate and Yogi got it and moved up and put the tag on him. But Bill Summers was the home-plate umpire and he called Jackie safe, and I thought Yogi'd go crazy. He jumped up and down with both feet off the ground at the same time, but they called him safe, anyway.

We won the second game, too, but then we went over to Ebbets Field and got screwed. In the first game there, they bombed Bob Turley in the first couple of innings and Campy hit one out off him. Mickey was still limping around but he asked Casey if he could play center, and he did. But he had trouble going after a fly ball, so the Old Man moved him over to right field for the rest of the game, and in the second inning he hit one over the center-field wall. But they beat us pretty bad, like 8 to 3.

The next day, Campy homered again off Don Larsen and Hodges hit one out, too. Finally, Snider hit one into Bedford Avenue, and I think he hit four homers off us in that Series. That time, they beat us, 8 to 5, but we were coming closer.

Then Casey started Bob Grim the next day, with the series tied up at two games each, and he gave up a couple of cheap homers to Sandy Amoros and Snider—no kidding, they just dropped over the fence and they looked like little pop flies. But later Snider hit one all the way out, and that was no cheapie, and they beat us again, 5 to 3, even though Yogi hit two homers for us late in the game.

When we went back to Yankee Stadium, we had to win a game just to stay alive. They used to say that Ebbets Field was no place for a left-handed pitcher, and not many ever beat the Dodgers there. I was pretty lucky because I only lost about two games there in my life. Well, maybe I was pretty lucky because I only pitched about two games there in my life. But I didn't pitch any games there that year, and Casey started me in the fifth game of the series back in the stadium. The Dodgers started Karl Spooner, who was a left-handed phenom, he struck out seventeen batters one time that summer and fifteen another time. But this time, he only struck out one of our guys, and it was the only out he got. We came up with a couple of singles, a couple of walks and then Moose put one out, and we got five runs and won it, 5 to 1.

Now we were all tied up in the seventh game, with Tommy Byrne pitching for us against Johnny Podres. And the Dodgers got ahead of us, 2 to 0, but in the sixth inning we got something going. Billy Martin led off with a walk, then McDougald got a bunt single, and up came Yogi. You wouldn't want anybody else in the world up then except Yogi, either.

Podres threw him a fast ball outside and Yogi hit it down the line in left field, sort of a high lob-shot that might've been a ground-rule double if it bounced, or maybe just a foul ball. Anyway, we figured all the Dodgers would be playing him around to right, but Amoros was "cheating" on him in left field and was playing a hell of a lot closer to the foul line than he should have. He kept running and getting closer to the low railing. He just kept running, and finally he stuck up his glove and made a fantastic catch. We couldn't believe it. Then we couldn't believe it when he whipped the ball to Pee Wee Reese, and he threw it on one hop all the way to Hodges, who doubled up McDougald at first.

That was the way it ended, too, 2 to 0. It was the first time the Dodgers ever won the Series and the first time we ever lost one since Casey became the manager. Mickey only played in three of the seven games, and the Old Man said later, "That was the difference." I think the Dodgers got almost $10,000 each for their winning share and we got $5,500 for our losing share. It was the first time we had to take the loser's share—$4,500 less—and *that* was the difference, too.

MICKEY:
Casey always asked me if I could play—he got the idea pretty early that my legs were bad, and some days they were

worse than others. Hell, in the first World Series I ever got in, it was 1951, my rookie year, I got hurt in the second game. It was right after the Giants won the pennant in the National League when Bobby Thomson hit the home run in the last inning of the playoff with Brooklyn. We already won our pennant by then and were just waiting for them to finish their playoff to see who'd get in the Series against the Yankees.

I remember that some of our guys even went up to the Polo Grounds that day just to watch the game. Yogi was one of them. But in the top of the ninth inning, the Dodgers were ahead of the Giants, 4 to 1, so Yogi decided he'd get out of there and beat the traffic home. Then Thomson hit the home run, and the Giants got four runs and won it in the last half of the ninth. And you know how everybody asks, Where were you when Bobby Thomson hit his home run? Well, Yogi was in his car driving home and he always used to grin and say, "I was listening on the car radio."

Anyway, the next day we were all in Yankee Stadium for the first game of the Series with the Giants, and I woke up like ten times tighter than when I played in my first big league game. But my father was there and we took a ride up Fifth Avenue, looking at all the buildings and stores, and I got calmed down. I was the lead-off man then and I didn't get a hit, and they beat us.

Then the next day, in the fifth inning, I was chasing a fly out in right-center, and most people don't remember it was Willie Mays who hit it. You know, it was his rookie year, too. I was getting ready to catch it, and Joe DiMaggio was already standing under it and he was hollering, "I got it." And you don't want to run into Joe DiMaggio. So I put on the brakes as hard as I could and my back spikes caught on this drain, they had this rubber drain cover in the outfield grass, and when my spikes caught it, my knee just went straight out. You know, I was scared stiff. Scared the hell out of me. I didn't know what happened, and they took me to the hospital and I got operated on.

People think I was always hurt, but I played eighteen years and got in more games than anybody else ever did for the Yankees. But I think Casey would always worry that I'd hurt myself doing some damned thing like kicking hell out of the water cooler in the dugout after I struck out. He'd watch me pull that shit and say, "If you get hurt, it's going to cost you plenty." One time I was all pissed off and kicking things, and he went over to the bat rack and pulled out one of the bats and told me, "Here, why don't you bang yourself on the head with this?"

Some of the guys used to get pissed off at Casey because he was always platooning them out of the lineup. But he was like a father to me, and if you want to know how he could handle people, with all that clowning that he'd do and all, just ask Ellie Howard how it was after he came up that year we were talking about, 1955 it was. He was the first black player the Yankees had, and it took him a long time to get there, he was already like twenty-six years old and he played with the Kansas City Monarchs in the Negro Leagues before the Yankees signed him.

I don't know why it took Ellie so long to make it to the ball club. Maybe because it usually took anybody a long time—the Yankees had so many strong players then that it was the toughest team to make, anyway. Some people said they also dragged their feet about signing black guys—the Yankees and the Boston Red Sox—but in the locker room we players never had any feeling that way.

After Jackie Robinson came up with the Dodgers, the American League got Larry Doby and then the Dodgers got Roy Campanella and Don Newcombe, and after that a lot of guys started showing up from the Negro Leagues. The Yankees signed Vic Power and Artie Wilson and Ruben Gomez and Frank Barnes, but Elston was the only one who got all the way to the big club.

He was voted the Most Valuable Player in the International League in 1954, and then the Yankees took him to spring training the next year. He was an outfielder and they made him into a catcher, but any team that had Yogi back there didn't need too much help catching. Ellie was a real gentleman, and he could hit and hit long, and he was good at everything except maybe running. Casey used to say, "When I finally get one, I get the only one in the world who can't run."

When he came up that season, it was eight or nine years after Jackie Robinson but there was still a lot of horseshit that black guys had to put up with, especially down South, like during spring training. We guys lived in one of the good hotels in St. Pete, but Ellie had to live down in the black section in south St. Pete; he stayed there with a Negro doctor, I think it was. He'd have to take a taxi to the ball park, but when he got there, Casey and everybody would try to treat him like anybody else. And if we took a trip by bus, if we stopped at a place where they'd make black people eat out back or in some other part of the restaurant, some of us would stay with him and eat on the bus.

I don't know how he did it, even though the Yankees never had any problems like that. I don't ever remember anybody treating him bad. Casey put him in the outfield for a while because Yogi was catching every day and he wanted Elston to play. He could hit and do everything, and he even got to calling Rizzuto "my Great White Father" because Rizzuto went out of his way to lead him around. And once I remember Elston won a game for us in the ninth inning, maybe it was the first time he did it, and so Rizzuto and me and some of the guys spread these towels all the way from the dugout into the clubhouse for him, like a Goddamned red carpet.

WHITEY:
Ellie had it tough the first few years, traveling around in the South and all. But one of the worst incidents I remember was sort of accidental. Casey hired Rudy York, you know, the

old hitter from the Tigers, to go around the league for us and do some scouting—he actually was supposed to steal the other clubs' signs, he was pretty good at picking up little things pitchers did that tipped off what they were throwing. We'd heard that Rudy had helped Hank Greenberg hit all those home runs, he was so good at picking up signs.

So we were in Baltimore once, and Casey hired out a room in the hotel so York could give us a scouting report, and Elston was the only black guy on the team. So Rudy York gets up in front of the team in this room, and he was from Alabama and didn't realize that Elston was with us now, and he starts to give us his report on the Orioles, who had a black guy pitching for them that night.

"Hi, fellows," he says. "Tonight Connie Johnson is pitching for Baltimore. And when he holds his full right hand right up in his glove, you know he's going to be throwing a fast ball. When he drops his hand down, and you can see the heel of it below his glove, it'll be a curve ball. You know, niggers have white palms—lighter than the backs of their hands. . . ."

By then, it was so quiet in the room, you could hear a pin drop. We were so embarrassed, with Elston sitting there and listening.

People still ask if the Yankees dragged their feet promoting black guys to the big team. Well, I thought they were slow bringing up Latin or black players. I started to think about it when we'd get hot scouting reports on Elston from places like Muskegon, Wisconsin. Then he went to Toronto and had a hell of a year up there. But the guys on the ball club never talked about it generally.

I did, though. Half my high school was black and a third Spanish. Don't forget, I lived in New York.

I don't remember any blacks in Norfolk in 1948, the year Larry Doby came up with the Cleveland Indians. But my first year at Binghamton, 1949, was my first year playing against blacks in the pros. There were three black players on Wilkes-

Barre in the Eastern League then: Roy Welmaher, a good left-handed pitcher, who was a little old by then. And Al Smith, the outfielder, who later played with Cleveland and the White Sox. And Suitcase Simpson, who came up in '51 with Cleveland.

We had a couple of red-necks screaming, "Do this, do that," or moaning that they wouldn't put up with that down South. But by then I'd seen some good players down in Mexico in the winter of 1948–49. Like Ray Dandridge, I played against him in Mexico then and in the American Association two years later—and he was great. Guys like Cannonball Mc-Daniels from Kansas City, who was a good friend of Satchel Paige, and Barney Sorell, and Marvin Williams, an infielder. Mala Torres, the father of Hector Torres, and a center fielder, was one of the best players I ever saw. He wouldn't leave Mexico, though, because he couldn't speak English.

This was the first winter after Jackie Robinson and Larry Doby broke in. And they had guys like Mike Garcia on the Indians in 1948 and Bobby Avila the next year. But we thought in Mexico that the guys we were playing against were as good as them.

I joined the Yankees in 1950 and never remember anybody yelling "You black bastards" or anything like that. Now and then something would happen, but color wasn't the big thing. I got pissed off at Luke Easter in one game. He hit a grounder down by first base to Johnny Mize, and it went through John's legs. Bobby Richardson who was backing up the play, fielded the ball and threw it to me as I was running to cover first. Easter knocked me twenty feet into right field.

Hell, he was six-foot-six and weighed two-fifty. But I ran after the ball and threw out Joe Gordon at third base. It was a big play. When Gordon saw the ball shoot out of my hand, he tried to go from first to third, but I threw him out. Everybody in the park, including Gordon, thought I was dead. I did have to leave the game a couple of innings later because my hip was hurting.

I remember that one of our pitchers, Jim Coates, who was from Virginia, had a little trouble with Vic Power. But Coates would knock you down whether you were black *or* white. And Billy Martin had some trouble with Doby. Once in Cleveland when Doby was batting, Art Ditmar chucked one over Doby's head and the ball went all the way back to the box seats. There was a man on second base, so Ditmar did what you're supposed to do after a wild pitch—he ran in and covered the plate. He was standing there waiting for the throw back from the catcher, and we saw Doby suddenly reach over and take a swing at him. Then all hell broke loose. Both teams got into this big brawl, with Doby on the bottom of the pile. Moose Skowron pulled him out by the legs, trying to work him free. But Billy and Doby yelled at each other for about five minutes.

I guess that a guy's color was the sensitive thing in those days, you know, for a few years after the Dodgers brought Jackie up. But they used to get on guys for other reasons, too.

Like the Yankees had two guys at opposite ends of the social scale, and you might take them or leave them, depending. At one extreme, we had Joe Pepitone. He didn't drink much, but he liked to sing and dance. It didn't bother me and Mickey that Joe acted up, though some of the older guys resented him. The thing everybody hated to see was that he had a lot of potential that he didn't use.

Then, at the other extreme, you had Bobby Richardson. He was religious and neat and even prim. Casey used to come out with those remarks sometimes about "you milkshake drinkers," but we respected Bobby as a person and as a ballplayer. Hell, he never bothered anybody with his religion. He wasn't even a little pain in the ass.

On July 9, 1958, hearings were held in Washington by the Subcommittee on Anti-trust and Monopoly of the Committee of the Judiciary of the United States Senate. The subcommittee was considering H.R. 10378 and S. 4070: to limit the anti-trust laws so as to exempt professional baseball, football, basketball and hockey. The chief witness was Charles Dillon Stengel.

SENATOR ESTES KEFAUVER: Mr. Stengel, you are the manager of the New York Yankees. Will you give us very briefly your background and your views about this legislation?

MR. STENGEL: Well, I started in professional ball in 1910. I have been employed in professional ball, I would say, for forty-eight years. I have been employed by numerous ball clubs in the majors and in the minor leagues.

I started in the minor leagues with Kansas City. I played as low as class-D ball, which was at Shelbyville, Kentucky, and also class-C ball and class-A ball, and I have advanced in baseball as a ball player.

I had many years that I was not so successful as a ball player, as it is a game of skill. And then I was no doubt discharged by baseball in which I had to go back to the minor leagues as a manager, and after being in the minor leagues as a manager, I became a major-league manager in several cities and was discharged, we call it discharged because there is no question I had to leave. [Laughter.]

And I returned to the minor leagues at Milwaukee, Kansas City, and Oakland, California, and then returned to the major leagues.

In the last ten years, naturally, in major-league baseball with the New York Yankees, the New York Yankees have had tremendous success and while I am not a ball player who does the work, I have no doubt worked for a ball club that is very capable in the office.

I have been up and down the ladder. I know there are some things in baseball thirty-five to fifty years ago that are better now than they were in those days. In those days, my goodness, you could not transfer a ball club in the minor leagues, class-D, class-C ball, class-A ball.

How could you transfer a ball club when you did not have a highway? How could you transfer a ball club when the railroads then would take you to a town you got off and then you had to wait and sit up five hours to go to another ball club?

How could you run baseball then without night ball?

You had to have night ball to improve the proceeds, to pay larger salaries, and I went to work, the first year I received $135 a month. I thought that was amazing. I had to put away enough money to go to dental college. I found out it was not better in dentistry. I stayed in baseball.

Any other questions you would like to ask me?

SENATOR KEFAUVER: Mr. Stengel, are you prepared to answer particularly why baseball wants this bill passed?

MR. STENGEL: Well, I would have to say at the present time, I think that baseball has advanced in this respect for the player help. That is an amazing statement for me to make, because you can retire with an annuity at fifty and what organization in America allows you to retire at fifty and receive money?

Now the second thing about baseball that I think is very interesting to the public or to all of us is that it is the owner's own fault if he does not improve his club, along with the officials in the ball club and the players.

Now what causes that?

If I am going to go on the road and we are a traveling ball club and you know the cost of transportation now—we travel sometimes with three Pullman coaches, the New York Yankees, and I am just a salaried man and do not own stock in the New York Yankees, I found out that in traveling with the New York Yankees on the road and all, that it is the best, and we have broken records in Washington this year, we have broken them in every city but New York and we have lost two clubs that have gone out of the city of New York.

Of course, we have had some bad weather, I would say that they are mad at us in Chicago, we fill the parks.

They have come out to see good material. I will say they are mad at us in Kansas City, but we broke their attendance record.

Now on the road we only get possibly twenty-seven cents. I am not positive of these figures, as I am not an official. If you go back fifteen years or if I owned stock in the club, I would give them to you.

SENATOR KEFAUVER: Mr. Stengel, I am not sure that I made my question clear. [Laughter.]

MR. STENGEL: Yes, sir. Well, that is all right. I am not sure I am going to answer yours perfectly, either. [Laughter.]

SENATOR JOSEPH C. O'MAHONEY: How many minor leagues were there in baseball when you began?

MR. STENGEL: Well, there were not so many at that time because of this fact: Anybody to go into baseball at that time with the educational schools that we had were small, while you were probably thoroughly educated at school, you had to be—we had only small cities that you could put a team in and they would go defunct.

Why, I remember the first year I was at Kankakee, Illinois, and a bank offered me $550 if I would let them have a little notice. I left there and took a uniform because they owed me two weeks' pay. But I either had to quit—but I did not have enough money to go to dental college—so I had to go with the manager down to Kentucky.

What happened there was if you got by July, that was the big date. You did not play night ball and you did not play Sundays in half of the cities on account of a Sunday observance, so in those days when things were tough, and all of it was, I mean to say, why they just closed up July 4 and there you were sitting there in the depot.

You could go to work some place else, but that was it.

So I got out of Kankakee, Illinois, and I just go there for the visit now. [Laughter.]

SENATOR JOHN A. CARROLL: The question Senator Kefauver asked you was what, in your honest opinion, with your forty-eight years of experience, is the need for this legislation in view of the fact that baseball has not been subject to anti-trust laws?

MR. STENGEL: No.

SENATOR CARROLL: I had a conference with one of the attorneys representing not only baseball but all of the sports, and I listened to your explanation to Senator Kefauver. It seemed to me it had some clarity. I asked the attorney this question, What was the need for this legislation? I wonder if you would accept his definition. He said they didn't want to be subjected to the *ipse dixit* of the federal government because they would throw a lot of damage suits on the *ad dammum* clause. He said, in the first place, the Toolson case was *sui generis,* it was *de minimus non curat lex.*

Do you call that a clear expression?

MR. STENGEL: Well, you are going to get me there for about two hours.

SENATOR KEFAUVER: Thank you, very much, Mr. Stengel. We appreciate your presence here.

Mr. Mickey Mantle, will you come around?

Mr. Mantle, do you have any observations with reference to the applicability of the anti-trust laws to baseball?

MR. MANTLE: My views are just about the same as Casey's.

BILLY'S BATTLEFIELD

MICKEY: Casey never got on us very much, considering everything that happened. Once in a while, when he was mad, he'd use us for a target. He'd say things about me and Billy mostly. Sometimes he'd call us into the office and say we were staying out too late or drinking too much, things like that. He was a hell of a philosopher, I thought, because he'd never pick on anybody going real bad on the ball field. Most of the time, he'd pick on guys who were going good. You know, he would use somebody who was having a good year to get on the other guys. And one time he was getting on us in a meeting in the clubhouse, getting on us about the drinking, and that's when we all got the nickname "Slick."

We was having a meeting this time, the whole ball club, and Casey was getting on me and Billy and Whitey, and at the end of his talk he was getting all tied up the way he did, you know. And he ended up saying, "Damn it, some of you guys are drinking so much you're getting whiskey-slick."

A lot of the guys didn't know what the hell he was talking about, and I didn't know what the hell he was talking about myself. But I knew who he was talking *to*, and it just so happened at that time that Billy and myself and Whitey were going pretty good. So that kind of stuck with us: *whiskey-slick*.

Really, I think that Whitey is called "Slick." He's slick on the mound, like he had a few little tricks that nobody ever knew about. Like throwing mud balls, and sneaky pick-off throws to first. Really like a . . . well, when I hear "Slick," I think about a carnival con artist or something. Whitey had a lot of that in him. A pretty good con artist, but he's so good-natured that people don't think of things he's liable to come up with.

I remember one time, me and Whitey missed a team bus or something, and we had to go between Baltimore and Washington around the Fourth of July, so we had to take a cab. And we stopped and got a bottle of scotch and some set-ups, and took off on our trip, Baltimore to Washington, to catch up to the team. And about halfway over there, Whitey spots a place on the side of the road selling fireworks, and hollers "Stop!"

Well, Goddamn, at that time I was making a hundred thousand a year and Whitey was making about seventy, and there was no sense in stealing some fireworks. But he goes up there like he's buying, you know, and he paid the guy five dollars and he just took a sack and he was sneaking them into the sack, and I'm setting in the cab watching him and I know there are a lot of cars standing around out there, and they had to be watching him, too.

Well, anyway, he got a bunch of Roman candles and all kinds of things, and he set one of the Roman candles off in the cab when he came back, and the driver was trying to dodge the damned Roman candle inside his cab.

Finally, we got to the hotel in Washington, and we set all of the fireworks off then, like we was starting a war or something up in the room. I remember that I had some real nice suits that I just bought, and they were hanging in the closet, but the closet door was open—and that stink was all over the place. Smoke and explosions and noise, and sparks were flying all over the place. It wrecked the rug and ruined my suits, so I finally opened the window in the room and then all the smoke went pouring out. It's a wonder we didn't get called in for a false alarm or something, the room was so shot up, and a couple of the ball players from other rooms came rushing up to see what the hell was going on.

Like I said, he was having some fun, thinking he was putting something over on somebody, and that's the kind of guy he was. Like a carnie or a slicker, or like maybe a city slicker. A lot of people also call me "Slick," because out of that same meeting that Casey called that day, I think all three of us got the name. But when you say "Slick," it's usually Whitey. He's the one everybody thinks of as "Slick."

Most of the time, me and Billy call each other names that this guy from Commerce gave us. Roy Crow, he might've been thirty years old but he always acted more like a little kid even though he weighed about two hundred and forty and had this baseball cap pulled down on his head all the time. He couldn't talk too plain, but everybody let him come and go into their houses, they all liked him, and I don't know how to explain it exactly but he called Billy "Bill Barton" and he called me "Pickey." And every time he'd come by, he would have a bunch of imaginary men with him. People who were his friends—Obin Jackson and Hal Tuna and guys like that. There was nobody there, but he would introduce you to them anyway, and once when Billy was with me down in Commerce, I had him introduce Billy Martin to all his imaginary friends. And Billy never forgot Obin Jackson, so now he always calls *me* "Obin," and I call him "Hal Tuna," who's really supposed to be somebody named Hal Turner in Roy's world. It was kind of sad, but we kept the nicknames, and that's probably why Whitey got stuck with "Slick" most of the time by himself.

––––––

Alfred Manuel Martin was born May 16, 1928, in one of the oldest houses still standing in Berkeley, California. His father was a Portuguese from the Hawaiian island of Maui. His mother was Italian, and she still lives in the house, though Mr. Martin left it eight months after Billy was born. As a teen-ager, all ears and nose, he was never called Alfred Manuel; he referred to himself as "the Dago" or "Por-to-gee," with a hard "g," and mostly he was known as Billy because his grandmother, who raised him, liked to call him *bello*—which meant that, in Italian at least, he was cute.

He signed with the Oakland Oaks of the Pacific Coast League when he was still in his teens, and the manager was Casey Stengel. Stengel was thirty-eight years older than Martin but it was a marriage of true minds. Martin had few visible talents as a baseball player outside of nerve and a sort of galloping case of *chutzpah*, and Stengel loved every snippy fibre in his wiry little body. And when Casey went up to the Yankees in 1949, he gave Martin one more season of ripening, then sent him a ticket to New York.

For most of the next seven and a half years, except for two when he was bedeviling the Army brass, Billy Martin was one of Stengel's most outrageous money players and probably his all-time pet. He hit twenty-nine home runs during that time, which was 178 fewer than Mickey Mantle hit. But he proved a hellcat in his five World Series, hitting .333 with five home runs and scoring fifteen runs and knocking in nineteen others in twenty-eight games. And he saved the 1952 Series with a sprinting, sprawling catch of a wind-blown pop fly hit by Jackie Robinson that five other Yankees watched, spellbound and sunstruck. But to George Weiss, who put together the Yankee teams of the 1950s and who watched them like a hawk from the front office, too much of Martin's dash took place off the field as the running mate to Mantle and Ford. By 1957, after Stengel's team had won seven pennants in eight years, Martin was privately rated "a bad influence" on Mantle in particular; by midsummer, he was gone. After that: six teams in five years. Later, he was hired—and fired—as the manager of the Minnesota Twins, Detroit Tigers and Texas Rangers, until he finally came home in 1975 to run the Yankees, one generation and many battles later.

BILLY MARTIN:

Weiss hated me. When I came up in 1950, my first day with the club, we were losing 9 to 0 in Boston and the Old Man put me in. The first time up, I doubled off the left-field fence in Fenway Park for one run, and later in the same inning I got a single with the bases loaded for two more. Two hits in the same inning, my first two times up. We won the game, 15 to 10, no kidding.

The Old Man liked me, I guess, because I was a lot like him, the way he was when he was young. I suppose I had a lot of balls for a rookie. But he was harder on me than on anybody. I may have been his pet, but Casey still demanded more of me on the field.

Weiss wanted to send me down that first year. He was trying to get rid of George Sternweiss but couldn't make the deal; so, until he did, he had to unload one other player to keep the roster at twenty-five, and he picked me. During all the fussing, I got to bat three times: The first time, I hit a three-run home run, another time I got a single, and the third time I got a walk. But he still insisted on sending me down to Kansas City for thirty days till they got Sternweiss straightened out.

Casey came to me and said he had to send me down for thirty days, then he said: "But why ain't you mad? If it was me, I'd squawk to him." So I did. I went to the office and told Weiss that I thought it was a hell of a thing, that I didn't deserve to go back to the minors and I could play with the Yankees, and all that. He really got pissed off at me for daring to argue it out with him. After that, even after he sent me down and I came back thirty days later, Weiss was always bugging me. He even had detectives following me in spring training, and he said: "If I catch you stepping out of line, you're gone."

I don't know if I stepped out of line or not, but I roomed with Mickey and we were always together. He was more than a friend to me, he was more like a brother, even closer than most brothers. I even spent one winter living with him and Merlyn back in Commerce, I guess it was 1953. I don't know what kind of influence I was on him, but he wasn't a bad influence on me—he was a good influence.

Hell, when I was at Oakland with Casey, he roomed me with Cookie Lavagetto. He was a lot older than me; he was on the way down from the big leagues, and he was more like my father. I'd come in at night holding my shoes in my hand so I wouldn't wake him up and get a lecture. But when Mickey and I roomed together on the Yankees, we did it like brothers. He always got up early, and he'd even order breakfast for the two of us while I was still sleeping. He got to know everything about me, like I had this crush on Debbie Reynolds in those days, going to all her movies and everything. And after I went in the Army, I got an autographed picture of Debbie Reynolds in the mail, signed "With all my love." Yeah, Mickey faked it up and sent it to me.

One Sunday we were in the hotel and he ordered eggs for breakfast. They always had to be three-minute eggs, but this time they were only done one and a half minutes, so he left them sitting there. In those days, it seemed that every time I threw something, I hit something. So I picked up his eggs and looked out the window and saw Vic Raschi and Rae Scarborough down on the street getting into a cab to go to church and then the ball park. We must've been fifteen stories above the street and I started to pitch his eggs out the window toward the street where they were getting into this cab.

Mickey tried to stop me; I still remember him shouting to me, "No, don't do it, Billy." But I let one egg fly, and you wouldn't believe it, the damned thing dropped fifteen floors and hit the cabbie right between the eyes and splattered all over Raschi and Scarborough. Damn. Then Mantle and I started piling chairs, tables and everything we could find—piling it up in front of the door like a blockade to keep them the hell out, because we knew they were heading up to the room to kick the shit out of us.

Another time, when the Yankees went to Japan after the season, we went to a lot of places with our wives and they finally said one night that Mickey and Whitey and I could go out on the town by ourselves, they'd just stay back in the hotel and take it easy. So I was supposed to pick them up at Whitey's room, and I got there while he was in the bathroom shaving. Joan was in bed, all tired out, when I got there. But I said to her, move over, and then I got on the other side of the bed on top of the covers and all, and I was all dressed, anyway. But I was lying there when Whitey got done shaving and came out of the bathroom, and I timed it right, so I was saying to her, "When will Whitey get back, Joanie?" And he broke up when he came in and spotted me lying there on the bed.

That's the way we guys lived together, like brothers, doing things to each other, hunting and fishing together, drinking together, being part of each other's families. Casey didn't mind too much what we did, but Weiss hated me. After I made that catch on Robinson in the Series, he even said, "You made an easy play look hard."

MICKEY:
Casey never had a curfew on us or anything like that, unless we got into a slump or started going bad on the field. But we must've made George Weiss wish to hell he had kept us locked up in our rooms sometimes.

Once in spring training, Whitey and me stayed back from a trip—you know, if the club was taking one of those long bus rides—like from St. Pete down the coast to where the Pirates used to train, Fort Myers, I think it was, three or four hours each way—you'd just as soon jake it and not go. This one time, the Yankees were going down there and I'd played in about every game so far and I didn't want to make that one. So I told Casey my shoulder was hurting, which it had been, but I guess I could've played if he wanted me to. So right away, Casey says fine, you can stay back.

Well, Whitey was already staying back because he wasn't supposed to pitch that day anyway, and we really wanted to play golf instead of going to Fort Myers. So the minute the bus got out of sight, me and Whitey jumped in the car and took off for Clearwater, where they had this beautiful golf course alongside that old resort hotel up there. And we were playing golf and having a hell of a time all afternoon—until we were walking down the fairway to the eighteenth green and I suddenly said, "Damn, doesn't that guy up there on eighteen look like George Weiss."

Then I remembered that Weiss used to stay at that hotel sometimes during spring training, and the closer we got to the green, the more the guy looked like Weiss. And Whitey said, "Yeah, it sure as shit does look like him." But by now we're getting close to the green so we just keep walking. Then we come up the little hill and, sure enough, it's him. There he is, looking out our way now and he spots us, and as we come up there he just gets redder in the face and says to me, "How's your shoulder?"

"Not too good, Mr. Weiss," I say. "I couldn't throw a ball very good with it, but it doesn't bother me when I swing the club." And he stares back at us and his face gets redder and redder, and he finally just turns without saying another word and stomps right the hell off the course.

But Casey didn't mind too much and he never put a curfew on us if the team was going good. Once he did, up in Boston, after we lost a few games and were dragging along. He had one of those team meetings of his and said we looked awful and we were drinking too much and all, so we better snap out of it and, until we do, there's an eleven-thirty curfew.

So that night, me and Billy go out for some dinner and we're sitting around the restaurant talking and all, and then we notice that the time's gone by and it's already half past eleven and we're late the first night the Old Man's got the curfew on. So we jump in a cab and hurry back to the hotel, the Kenmore, and we go rushing up the front steps to the lobby—and standing right there inside the door talking to some writers and some other guys was Casey.

We turned right around and got the hell out of there, because there's no way you can get in the lobby without going past him. But they had this back door to the Kenmore that you could reach through an alley—we used to go through it to get on the bus to go to Fenway Park. So me and Billy go shooting down the alley to the back door, but it's locked so you can't get in from the outside.

But Billy sees this here little window over the door and he says to me, "Boost me up and I'll go in through the window and open the door from inside." So I get down and he climbs up on my back and puts his feet on my back and shoulders and all, and steps all over me but finally pulls himself up and forces his way through the little window. I'm still there in the alley, but I think, Okay, it was worth it, he'll open the door and we'll be in. But I must've waited ten minutes without anything happening and I wonder where the hell he went. Then I hear him calling me and I look up and there's Billy at the window, saying to me, "It's locked on the inside. I'll see you later." And then he disappears, and I'm still standing down there in the alley thinking, That son of a bitch, he'll just go on to bed and leave me out here.

I know I can't go back through the lobby out front, and now it's good and late anyway. But they've got all these garbage and trash cans stacked out in the alley so the trash people can pick up the stuff in the morning, and I figure out that I'll pile them up and get in through the little window, too. So I put a few cans together and climb up on them, and by now

I'm getting garbage all over my suit and everything, and I'm scraping my hands and getting all messed up. But finally I pull myself up and get my shoulder in the window and somehow get through it and sneak up to the room, looking like I got hit by a garbage truck. And when I get there, all steamed up and pissed off, there's Billy in the room without a care in the world, laughing his Goddamned head off.

He would've left me standing out there all night—that's the way he was, nothing like that ever bothered him, even with old Casey standing in the lobby by the front door.

But that's the way we lived, like we were in the same family, until Billy got traded to Kansas City in 1957.

WHITEY:

It was Billy's birthday, and Mickey and I were going to take him out to celebrate. We invited Yogi and Johnny Kucks and Hank Bauer, and there was Mickey and me and Billy, and all of our wives. We went to the Copacabana and Sammy Davis, Jr. was the entertainer there, and we had a big table, we must've had twelve or maybe fourteen people around it.

Over on the other side of the room was another big table, we found out later it was a bowling team, some husbands and wives on a bowling team, and they were getting into the sauce pretty good and they were hollering out things to Sammy Davis. He was pretty well known then but not as well known as he is now. They were hollering out things like, "Sing this, Black Sambo," and rough things like that. So finally Bauer asked them to be quiet, and they came back with some snotty remark, and we let it go for awhile. But they kept it up, and Bauer finally said, "Okay, knock it off over there."

Somebody over there answered, "Well, why don't you make me." So Bauer got up and the guy said something like, "Come on in the back," and started heading for the back of the place. Billy went back there, too, and then all the rest of the men at our table got up and went toward the back. We got there maybe ten or fifteen seconds later, and by then the guy that told Bauer to come into the back was stretched cut on the floor.

Bauer was a tough-looking guy who'd been in the Marines, and you know what Billy was like. But I know Bauer didn't hit him, or Billy, either, because they never left our sight, they were just forty or fifty feet in front of us all the time. And the guy was stretched out when we got there. He looked like he'd been hit fifteen times.

We cleared out of the place with our wives then, but the next day Roy Hamey called and said to get right over to the Yankees' office. It got in all the papers by then, and I remember Hamey saying, "You be over to this office in a half-hour; you're fined a thousand dollars and, if you're not here in a half-hour, it'll double." I said, well, there was no way that I could get from Glen Cove, where we were living on Long Island, into the Yankee office at 745 Fifth Avenue in a half-hour. But I went, anyway, to see what the hell it was all about.

Well, anyway, they fined us all a thousand dollars: it was Yogi and Bauer and Kucks, and Mickey, Billy and I, and one other guy—Gil McDougald, it was—there were seven of us. They only fined Johnny Kucks five hundred dollars because it was his rookie year. The next day, Dan Topping had us all meet the Yankees' lawyer up at the stadium, and we walked into the office and we told the exact story, that we just went to the back of the Copa and by the time we got there, the guy was stretched out on the floor. So the lawyer said, well, just tell that story to the grand jury just like you told me. And that was the first we heard about the grand jury.

The whole meeting with the Yankees' lawyer took only ten minutes. Then a while later, we went down to appear before the grand jury because this guy that started it all was pressing charges. Mickey was the first one, standing in the middle of the jury room and people asking him questions. I'll never forget it, Mickey was chewing gum and some lady on the grand jury said, "Are you chewing gum, Mr. Mantle?" And he says, "Yes, M'am." She said, "Would you mind getting rid of it?" So Mickey looks around and there's no place to put it there, he was standing in the middle of the room out in the open. So he took the gum out of his mouth and held it in his fingers the whole time the grand jury was questioning him.

We each went in and told the exact same story, you know, of what happened. And the grand jury finally threw the case out. But we still got fined by the club. And something I'll never understand is the lawyer's fee, which was $7,000, and we all had to add another thousand or so, besides being fined, to pay that.

The whole thing was something I could never understand. We were in the Copa watching the show, and some guy gets belted, and it ends up costing us $2,000 apiece. It got a lot of publicity, naturally. Everybody thought Billy or Hank hit the guy. He was a delicatessen owner from the Bronx, and he said Bauer hit him. Who did hit him? I guess it was one of the guys who worked at the Copa. If it had been Hank or Billy, we would've seen it, we weren't out of each other's sight the whole time.

I don't think we should've been fined, except for being out late. It pissed us off. We even had an off-day the next day, I think we were taking the train to Kansas City or St. Louis and, hell, the latest it could've been—if Sammy Davis was still doing his show—the latest his show could've been over was maybe one or one-thirty in the morning. So it wasn't even that late, anyway.

McDougald, who was Bauer's roommate then, got real mad when they fined us. He kept saying, "Nobody can tell me where I can or can't take my wife for an evening out." And when they asked Yogi who did what, he said, "Nobody did nothin' to nobody." But Casey got off the best one. He just said, "The reason they held the party there in that place was that they didn't want to hold it in a hospital."

Billy wasn't guilty that time, but the Copa thing gave Weiss a chance to trade him. You know, he figured he finally had a reason. And a month later, he sent him over to Kansas City. It was a sad day when Mickey and I found out that Billy got traded. He was sitting in the bullpen and in the middle of the game, it was June 15th and we were in Kansas City. Casey got him on the phone and said, "We want to talk to you." A few minutes later in the clubhouse, he told Billy, "We traded you to Kansas City." I think it was a Friday or Saturday, but anyway, we sat up all night, the three of us, and we drowned our feelings and talked all night long.

Billy couldn't get over it. He just said, "My birthday was May 16, and June 15 I'm gone. How can you be a bad influence on six pennant-winners?"

A week or so later, Kansas City came to New York to play us. They had Billy in their lineup now. And I remember I was pitching and had a big lead, like 8 or 9 to 0 going into the top of the ninth, and Billy got up and I threw him a big, slow curve. He took it for a strike, and as I'm winding up for the next one, I hollered in to him, "Same pitch." And I threw him another big, slow curve, and he hit it into the seats.

Stengel got very annoyed with me. I mean, the game was really over when it happened, but he still got pissed off that I told Billy what was coming. But I was kind of glad he hit it out. Billy claims to this day that I didn't tell him what was coming, and that's okay with me.

MICKEY:

For a long time after that, Billy wouldn't talk to Casey. He knew that Weiss really was the one who traded him because he was out gunning for him anyway, but Billy still felt Casey must've agreed to it. He said that was one time he needed Casey, and Casey didn't help him. And even though he always had been Casey's favorite player, he couldn't forgive him because he got traded away from the Yankees.

He kept it up, too, for several years. Whenever we'd play whichever team Billy was on then, he still wouldn't come over and talk to Casey. But I knew they were both hurting over it, so I kept trying to get them back together.

Finally, one day I went to Billy when his team was playing the Yankees and I said, "Billy, you've got to quit this and get back with Casey. He loves you like a son, the Old Man does, and he didn't trade you, anyway. Look, you're a lot younger than he is and one of these days he'll be gone and you'll regret it. You know he always gave you the chance to play and you were always his pet. Come on, it's sad for Casey to have you turning your back on him now."

And Billy listened and finally said okay, so I led him over to Casey in the dugout and they shook hands. Billy had tears in his eyes and he was crying, and the Old Man had tears in his eyes and he was starting to cry. And I had tears in my eyes, too, and I was crying. We were all standing there crying after everything we'd done together.

THE GREATEST
SHOW ON EARTH

WHITEY: Everybody thinks the Yankees were just one big happy family that got together in Florida every March to check the signals, drink and chase around all summer wherever the schedule happened to take us, and who got together again in New York every October to open the champagne and collect the World Series checks.

But it wasn't that simple. There were always seven other teams of guys in the league trying to beat us to the money, and eight teams in the other league lining up to get a crack at us, too. And sometimes they did, the way the Dodgers did in 1955.

We were big enough and happy enough, I guess. And most of the time, we were even like a family—or maybe a traveling circus. Like in spring training, when Billy Martin was rooming with Darrell Johnson downtown in St. Pete with the ball club, and Mickey and I were living out at Reddington Beach with our own families, a few doors away from each other.

In the back of our garage, Joan and I had a spare bedroom that we never used. I mean, we never used it till the night Darrell and Billy banged on our front door about one o'clock in the morning. I went and answered the door and found them there, and said, "What the hell's the matter?" And they said something like, "It's after curfew, Slick, we can't go back to the Soreno."

Now, to give you the picture, the Yankees used to take a bunch of rooms in a hotel for all spring training. They did it in St. Pete over on the Gulf coast of Florida, and they did the same thing after they moved their training headquarters to Fort Lauderdale on the Atlantic side. (That was in 1962, I guess, because that's when the Mets started in business and they took over our old place in St. Pete.) Anyway, they'd take maybe a couple of dozen rooms for the players who didn't have their wives with them and some of the coaches and writers and whoever else was traveling with the ball club. If you were a rookie, you had to stay at the hotel, but the other guys, especially if they had their families with them, could make their own deals for apartments or houses, and most of the time they'd find a place to live on the beach, which is what Mickey and I and our wives were doing when Martin and Johnson came banging on the door.

So I told them, okay, come on in. And Joan got some blankets out and some sheets and pillows, and they slept in the garage bedroom that night. Then the next morning, they went out to the ball park with me and Mickey.

That was okay, but the next thing we knew, Martin and Johnson started showing up all the time, staying in our garage and even keeping their Goddamned car in there. Our kids loved it. Eddie and Tommy were only three and four then, and Sally Ann was five. And I'd tell them in the morning, Go out and wake up Uncle Billy and Darrell, and they'd do it—with their water pistols. Billy even bought Tommy his first pair of cowboy boots then, and now Tommy's twenty-one and he still wears boots.

I've heard of a lot of ways of beating a curfew, but that may've been the best. It was a hell of an arrangement for Billy and Darrell. And I *knew* we were one big happy family when Joan came to me and wanted to know if she had to cook breakfast for them, too.

I guess we covered for each other all the time in those days. Once before a World Series game, I think it was in Milwaukee, a photographer came up to Mickey on the field and said, "Whitey, I'd like your picture winding up and following through." I didn't think we *looked* alike, but I was standing next to Mickey and slipped him my glove, so he went through it all for the guy—winding up, letting the ball fly, following through and all, and he did it left-handed like me, even though he threw righty.

And as stupid as he looked, winding up left-handed and all, the photographer took his pictures and ran them in the paper the next day with a caption that said something like, "Ford's famous windup." I got hold of a bat and offered to pose for the guy showing him "Mantle's famous swing," but for some reason Mickey didn't think that was so funny.

That's the way we always horsed around, though; we didn't have to rehearse it or anything, just sort of fell into it because we didn't go around worrying if the other guy was going to get pissed off. Maybe it was because of Casey and all the other characters we had on the team. Maybe because all the characters were good ball players, and we kept winning while we kept horsing around.

Like I said before, they always came up with players when we needed them, too, like Johnny Mize. Hell, he was already a big star when the Yankees got him from the Giants back in 1949, which was Casey's first season. Johnny was thirty-six then and he already had led the National League four times in home runs with the Cardinals. I think he finally hit around .359 or something, and we got him when Leo Durocher started phasing out the older guys on the Giants. He stayed with the Yankees five years, and he led them in pinch hitting three of the five years. Once he got seventy-six hits in a season, I think it was '50, my first year, and he batted in seventy-two runs, that's how valuable he was.

Maybe it was no coincidence that Mize's five years turned out to be the five years the Yankees won the World Series, the five straight. His last one was '53, and it was kind of sad because John was forty then and he mostly sat on the bench. But it was funny as hell, too, because he sat on the bench next to me when I wasn't pitching and he'd make a running commentary on everything that was happening.

We were playing the Dodgers, and it was my first season back from the Army. In the first game, it was at the stadium, they pitched Carl Erskine but he didn't last long. He walked three guys, and then Billy and Bauer got a couple of triples off him and we got four runs in the first inning. But a couple of days later, in Ebbets Field, Erskine set a World Series record by striking out fourteen of our guys. He even got Joe Collins and Mickey about four times each, he was so good with that big curve of his.

All the time Erskine's doing it, Johnny Mize is sitting next to me on the bench getting worked up, and he keeps saying, "They've got to stop swinging at that big overhand curve in the dirt, God damn it. Make him bring it up, bring it up." And the more he keeps saying it, the more Erskine keeps throwing it, and the more our guys keep missing it.

You can just imagine what finally happened. In the ninth inning, Casey sent Big John up to pinch-hit, and by then Erskine needed one more strikeout to break the Series record of thirteen. And Mize swung at one of those overhand curves that bounced in the dirt—and he was Number Fourteen.

MICKEY:

Everything seemed to happen to us in the World Series in those days, probably because if you screwed up then, you couldn't ever get it back. Like in '51, when Willie Mays hit that fly ball and I tore my knee trying to pull up so Joe DiMaggio could catch the ball. And in '52, when Billy made his catch running in on the infield grass. And the next year, when Erskine struck out all our guys but we still won it.

But the thing was, we kept getting new guys on the club, maybe one or two each year, and we always had something going to make sure we got into the Series. You had to fight to keep your job, too, whoever the hell you were. They were always wondering who ''the next Joe DiMaggio'' was going to be. And hell, there just wasn't any ''next DiMaggio.'' I remember they were always talking about me or somebody else like that, and one day I was out in the circle on deck and Joe Collins was batting, and he hit one way the hell and gone in the upper deck. It must've gone 450 feet, and when he crossed the plate and passed me where I was waiting to hit next, he said to me, ''Go chase that.''

Then I got up and hit one in the upper deck, too, only maybe it was farther out in the outfield and landed way the hell back in the seats. So I trotted around, then went into the dugout and shook hands the way you do, and then I went over to the water cooler and took a long drink. While I was doing it, Joe Collins was sitting there, so I stopped drinking for a minute and said to him, ''What did you think of that one, Joe?'' And he just sort of growled, ''Go shit in your hat.''

After we finally got beat in a Series—that was in 1955 by the Dodgers—we were lucky because we didn't have too much time to go around feeling sorry for ourselves. Right after we got beat, we took off for Japan on one of those tours. You know, every other year a different ball club was invited to play over there. They started going over way back when Babe Ruth and Lou Gehrig and those guys were playing, and after the war they started going over again. I think that Lefty O'Doul took an all-star team there like in 1951, and they won maybe thirteen games or so and only lost one, and they had a couple of ties because the Japanese had a time limit on the games. The Giants went in '53, and only got beat one game. And Eddie Lopat took another all-star team over that same year, and they won eleven out of twelve.

So now in '55, they invited us to go over, and it was sort

of a pain in the ass after playing all year long from back in February in Florida and all. But most of the guys had never been anywhere near Japan, so it was kind of exciting, too. They paid our way over and you got $5,000 if you went by yourself, I mean without bringing your wife, and $3,500 if she went with you. They took out $1,500 to pay her expenses.

But you know, even though a lot of funny things happened to us, it all started getting to you. I mean, here it was in late October and I'd been living in New York all summer without my family, and we had to pack and leave for Japan right after losing the Series. Merlyn was pregnant, so she didn't make the trip with me. We stopped in Honolulu to play a couple of games and had a ball there, then we flew to Tokyo, and by that time I was missing her and getting sort of homesick.

After about a week over there, I decided the hell with it. So I tried to figure out a way to get back home without getting Casey and the people there pissed off at me. What I did was to telephone this friend of mine in Commerce, this guy named Harold Youngman who used to help me look after my money and all. You'd call him my adviser, but he was really a good friend of mine back home who helped me manage some things. I called him and told him to send this here telegram, and to say in it that I had to rush right home because Merlyn was going to have the baby any minute.

I told Slick about it, but nobody else. And now the telegram arrives and I go to Casey and say, look, the baby's going to come any minute and Merlyn wants me home right away. So the Old Man says, why sure, you better get your ass on a plane and go home. And so that's how little David was born—the following February, which was like four months later.

Nobody seemed to mind it too much because they didn't know what happened till four months later. But Ford Frick was the commissioner then and he didn't think it was so funny. He fined me a thousand dollars.

WHITEY:

In the ball games over in Japan, they had these like Geisha girls waiting at home plate whenever one of the guys would hit a home run. They'd be there waiting with a present, one of those big Japanese dolls enclosed in a glass case. Andy Carey had a hot series there and hit about eleven home runs, and we all went home like pack-horses loaded down with the stuff.

There was one game we played there, and we had won like fifteen games in a row at that point, but this day the score was tied and the pitcher for their club was Kaneda, who was the Cy Young of Japan. He had won three or four hundred games. Anyway, this day I was pitching for the Yankees against him.

In the first inning, I walked a batter and then tried to pick him off first and threw it wild, so he got to second. Then Billy Martin put on the pick-off play at second base—you know, he gave the sign and all, he was going to teach them how we do the pick-off at second base. But I wheeled around and threw the ball too soon to Billy. I was supposed to count, then turn and throw it to the bag, but I didn't give Billy enough time to run over and sneak in behind the guy.

But I threw it anyway and the umpire was standing behind second base on the grass, and the ball hit him right on the forehead. No kidding, it ricocheted all the way over to the right-field line and the guy scored before Billy could run the ball down and throw it home. So they scored, and that was all they got because Don Larsen and I pitched a no-hitter. We scored one run, too, and it ended up in a tie, and it was the only game we didn't win in Japan.

I'll tell you the thing I remember most about that pick-off, though. It was when the ball hit the umpire right between the eyes—and he didn't flinch or even blink, as far as I could see. It was like nothing happened. He just turned around and watched Billy chasing the ball down the right-field line. Later, Gil McDougald came to me and said, ''Whitey, that's a tip-off on how hard you throw—when you hit a guy dead center from sixty feet away and he don't even change his expression."

When we got to Hiroshima, the ball club was still a little worried about the bomb being dropped there and how the people might be resenting us. So they asked us to stay in the hotel at night and not go out around the town. We always used to stay on the upper level of the hotel, anyway, where they usually had a cocktail lounge. And one night in Hiroshima, the guys were staying up late naturally and not going out, like they asked us to. Practically the whole team was there, and I guess we were getting pretty noisy after a while because around two or three o'clock in the morning, Stengel comes running out of his room in those bright red pajamas of his. And Charlie Silvera, who was pretty tanked on Japanese beer by then, hollered to him, "Where in hell's your reindeer, Santa Claus?"

Can you picture Casey Stengel standing there in red pajamas, looking like old man Mose with that great face of his and trying to quiet down a bunch of guys who were trapped in a hotel drinking all night? I don't think he was going to do anything about all the racket till Silvera started getting on him. So then Casey got pissed off and sent us all to bed for the night.

Another time—this was after Mickey pulled his fake-telegram trick, too—we went on a road trip from Tokyo to southern Japan, and the wives stayed back in Tokyo, with Edna Stengel and Hazel Weiss looking after them. Meanwhile, we played a game in a town that had an American Air Force base in it, I think it was Fukioka, and after the game we had a party at the hotel, naturally, and we invited all the officers and their wives from the airbase.

We had a hell of a time, and about two or three o'clock in the morning, most of the team had gone to bed and the officers and their wives had left, too. But a few of us were still there drinking—me and Billy Martin and Don Larsen and Eddie Robinson, and we still wanted to keep the party going but we didn't know how to get enough guys back to give it a boost, you know.

So we came up with this bird-brained idea to get everybody the hell out of the sack and get them back to the party.

What we did was to call Bob Fishel, the Yankee PR man, on the phone in his room and say, "You better get down here right away because some of the officers got mad because we were flirting with their wives, and we're having a big brawl down here." While I was saying this on the phone, Robinson and Martin and Larsen were banging the chairs and tables to make it sound as if there was a real big fight going on. And of course, Bob Fishel panicked over that—he was a good, straight guy, and I guess all he could imagine was big headlines in Tokyo and New York with photos and a diplomatic incident about us tearing up the hotel after a brawl with a lot of officers from the airbase.

It worked, too. Fishel came tearing down to see what the hell was happening and, meantime, we were busy phoning other players and giving them the same story. And before you know it, we had about twenty of the guys back downstairs at about four in the morning and we got the party going again full blast. We wound up paying for all the extra drinks and then we stayed for breakfast, too, so I think we had to shell out about fifty thousand yen. I can still see Bob running down from his room all upset that somebody was picking on his ball players. He was all ready to start swinging to help us out—dashing into the room downstairs in *his* pajamas, the way Casey did a few nights before.

We were pretty lucky because we might've started a couple of riots in Japan if the people hadn't been so good-natured and if Casey and Bob Fishel hadn't kept trying to get us out of trouble. We were lucky another way, too—before we got to Tokyo. I remember Casey got the team together and tried to talk us into taking the trip seriously and not screwing around too much. He said something like we were going to show the Japanese how we play this game, what it's all about, right? "And you fellows are going to perform 100 percent," he said, "because your jobs next year will depend on how well you do over there. So you'll be hustling, you'll be winning, you'll be trying to earn a job for next year."

We didn't know how serious the Old Man was, but remember—we didn't take too many chances those days because if we stopped winning, we might have to stop horsing around at night. I think we wound up winning twenty-three games and losing none, and they only tied us that once when my pick-off throw to Billy hit the Japanese umpire.

I'll tell you one thing, if you think it was fun traveling around with Casey, you should've seen him when his wife was along. Edna was a tall, good-looking woman who dressed magnificently; you know, they had a fair amount of money anyway because her family owned a bank in Glendale where they lived in California, and they owned apartment houses and Casey put money in oil wells in the thirties with Al Lopez and some other old ball players, and no kidding, they struck oil. They really struck oil. But Edna was a beauty. She kept their accounts because once she had been a bookkeeper, and she had even acted in the silent movies. Casey'd end up a speech sometimes by turning to her and saying, "And tell them about the time you played with Hoot Gibson."

She took a lot of trips with us because they always lived in the same big house in Glendale ever since they got married, I think it was back in 1924 or something, and she'd have to keep crisscrossing the country just to join him in New York every summer. And back home she kept their house filled with things they bought all over the world. They had a Chinese room upstairs and Japanese beds, and stuff like that.

One thing she didn't like was when people would say Casey was a funny old guy—you know, just a clown. She hated it the same way that Carmen Berra hated for people to make fun of Yogi's looks. Edna would always say, "He's not a clown. He's one of the smartest men in baseball, in business, in anything he'd try.'' And she'd remember that Casey used to ask her to find a job in the family's businesses for one of his old ball players. She'd say that on trips he might yell and holler and even insult her in front of the whole ball club, but she said he always quieted down thirty minutes later and got all sweet and courtly to her—and she was right.

Once she kept a team plane waiting because they couldn't find her "exit visa" or something, and the Old Man got all embarrassed because if it was a player that kept us waiting, Casey would've hit the ceiling. But this time it was his own wife, so he was embarrassed, and he started getting on her for it. On the airplane, he bitched and yelled at her, and then he sat there without saying anything for a few hours—you know, letting it sink in and all. He was pretty rough, and she just sat there all red in the face and took it.

When we finally landed, they had this chartered bus to take us to the hotel. But by then, Casey was beginning to feel a little sorry that he'd been so rough on her. So now he starts acting super-polite, like trying to make it up to her after all the hollering. They got on the bus and sat in the two front seats where the manager always sat, then he said, "I'll check and see that your bags are okay," so he hopped down from the bus and went around to where the guy was loading the bags in the hatch on the side of the bus.

Then he came back after a long while—I guess he was trying to show her that he was going to a lot of trouble being sweet and all—and he said, "Yeah, they're all right. They got all three of them packed in."

I guess that's what Edna had been waiting for—sitting there taking all that guff from him for a few hours. Now she finally gets a shot at him. She didn't change her expression or anything, or even look at him. She just waited a minute and then said, all nice and even and cool, as if he had just screwed up for real, "I had four."

Whenever we'd get new guys on the club, they couldn't believe the way it was—you know, we were a pretty loose bunch, and the Old Man was as loose as you could get. The biggest deal we ever made, I mean the biggest number of guys involved in a trade, was that year we went to Japan. Actually, it was in the winter before, so the guys we picked up in the deal made the trip with us. I think there were seventeen guys who got traded—eight came to the Yankees and nine went to the Baltimore Orioles. George Weiss was doing the talking for the Yankees and Paul Richards for the Orioles, so that should give you the idea.

We gave Baltimore guys like Harry Byrd and Gus Triandos and Willy Miranda, and my old pal Gene Woodling went, too, and Jim McDonald, Bill Miller, Hal Smith, Don Leppert and a third baseman we had, Kal Segrist. It turned out to be a pretty slick deal for the Yankees, because we got Don Larsen and Bob Turley, and right there it was a good deal because they could really pitch. But we also got another pitcher named Mike Blyzka, and Darrell Johnson, who was a catcher when he wasn't bunking in my garage in Florida with Billy Martin, and who later got to be manager of the Boston Red Sox. And we got Dick Kryhoski, who played first, and Billy Hunter and a couple of outfielders who went to the minors, Ted del Guercio and Tim Fridley. Unbelievable: seventeen guys in one deal.

I'll tell you what happened, and it's one reason the Yankees kept winning in the fifties, getting guys like that to take the place of the Allie Reynoldses and Vic Raschis and Eddie Lopats. Those two pitchers we got, they would've made the difference by themselves, Larsen and Turley. When they were with Baltimore, just before we made the trade, Turley won fourteen games and lost fifteen, I think it was; and the first year he was with the Yankees, he improved it to seventeen and thirteen. And Larsen, no fooling, he won only three games for the Orioles in 1954 and lost twenty-one. That's right, lost twenty-one. But with us, he was 9 and 2, and then 11 and 5, and you know what he did in the 1956 World Series with that perfect game he pitched.

After the trade, we started to win the pennant that season. You know, we won the five straight, then we finally lost one in '54 to the Indians. Then we started winning again in '55. Turley could throw bullets, and he won his seventeen games, but then he got stuck there. He was busting his ass trying to win twenty, but he lost three or four in a row. This was after he started the season winning eight out of nine and pitching a one-hitter and a two-hitter. But now he got stuck at seventeen, and he couldn't get over the hump and he started getting depressed and everything.

Turley was from some little town in Illinois, and he never drank or smoked, which wasn't too common on the Yankees in those days. But when we were leaving Chicago late in the season, getting on the train we guys loaded a whole case of beer, like it was standard traveling equipment, and I said to him, "Come on, Bob. Have a beer and forget it." So finally he had one, and the next thing you know, he had three or four.

He didn't make it to twenty games that year, but he did do it a couple of years later. And by then, he was one of the bunch—our one big happy family—on the field, on the train, wherever we went. And I reminded him about it later. I wasn't the team's philosophy teacher or anything, I guess I was just being kind of smart. But I told him, "Hell, if I didn't drink or smoke, I'd win twenty every year. It's easy if you don't drink or smoke or horse around."

HOW TO STRIKE OUT
WILLIE MAYS

During the golden Yankee years, it took 154 games to complete a schedule for one summer, and later 162 games. Between them, Whitey and Mickey appeared in 2,899 games. But no other roommates appeared in more "main events": eighty-seven games in a dozen World Series, and six All-Star games for Ford, sixteen for Mantle.

That was when they crossed the line from the American League to the National and matched talents with the "big boys" there: Jackie Robinson, Willie Mays, Henry Aaron, Warren Spahn, Sandy Koufax, Don Drysdale, Stan Musial. When the stakes seemed modest—as in the mid-season All-Star game, an extravaganza that stirred the public and flattered the players—their performance seemed modest. Ford pitched six times, allowed eleven earned runs in twelve innings, lost two games and won none. Mantle went to bat forty-three times, got eight singles and two home runs, batted in four runs, walked nine times and struck out sixteen times.

But in the World Series, with the money on the line, the Yankees grappled. From 1950 through 1964, Ford pitched in twenty-two games, allowed only forty-four runs in 146 innings for an earned-run average of 2.71, and won ten games and lost eight. Mantle got fifty-nine hits in 230 times at bat, including eighteen home runs; he knocked in forty runs and scored forty-two. Big boys against big boys.

WHITEY:

They played the All-Star game in San Francisco in 1961, and that was okay with us. You know, if you have three days "off" in the middle of the baseball season, you might as well spend them in San Francisco. In fact, they played the game on Tuesday and we got there on Monday, so Mickey and I headed right for the golf course. It was a place where the owner of the San Francisco Giants, Horace Stoneham, was a member and we played with his son, Peter. But we didn't have any equipment with us, no golf shoes or sweaters or anything. So Pete Stoneham said, "Just sign my father's name," and that was the best offer we'd had in a long time.

We didn't go so far as to buy golf clubs, but we did get new shoes, a pack of sweaters, balls and shirts, and the whole bill came to something like two hundred dollars. But Pete Stoneham insisted, "Just sign my father's name to it," and so we signed.

During the match, Joe DiMaggio and Lefty O'Doul were playing behind us in a twosome, a real San Francisco twosome, and the ninth hole was on an elevated green where I guess they couldn't see us from the fairway. Anyway, Mickey was getting ready to putt, and this ball came flying down and hit him right on the head, sort of glanced off his head while he was lining up his putt. Mickey thought for a minute that he'd been hit by a bullet, he dropped so fast to the ground. Then he realized it was a golf ball that just glanced off his head, either O'Doul's or DiMaggio's, I'm not sure—and neither one of them would admit who hit it, anyway.

Well, Toots Shor had a suite over in one of the big hotels in San Francisco, and he invited me and Mickey over for a little cocktail party he was having that night. That's one thing about Toots: Wherever he happened to light for the evening, you could bet your ass he'd be surrounded by a lot of people, and you could also bet your ass the people would be surrounded by a lot of cocktails.

So we were there telling everybody about our golf game, and how Mickey got hit on the head by a ball. And while they were all talking, I went over to Horace Stoneham to pay back the two-hundred-dollar tab that we ran up at his club. I explained to him that we'd signed for everything in sight and here was his two hundred bucks back.

Horace is a nice generous man who's free with his booze and his money, and he didn't seem to want to take the dough back. You know, he looked sort of amused at the way we took him up on his offer. So he said, "Look, I'll make a deal with you. If you happen to get in the game tomorrow and you get to pitch to Willie Mays, if you get him out we'll call it even. But if he gets a hit off you, then we'll double it—you owe me four hundred, okay?''

So I went over to Mickey and told him what Horace said, but Mickey wouldn't go for it. No way. He knew that Mays was like 9 for 12 off me lifetime, and he didn't have any reason to think I was going to start getting Willie out now, especially in his own ball park. But I talked him into it, since we had a chance to get out of it without paying Horace anything, and he finally said all right. Now all I had to do was get Willie out.

Sure enough, the next afternoon in Candlestick, there I am starting the All-Star game for the American League, with Warren Spahn pitching for the National. Willie's batting clean-up, and in the first inning I got the first two guys out, but then Roberto Clemente clipped me for a double—and there comes Willie.

Well, I got two strikes on him somehow, and now the money's on the line because I might not get to throw to him again.

So I did the only smart thing possible under the circumstances: I loaded the ball up real good. You know, I never threw the spitter—well, maybe once or twice when I needed to get a guy out really bad. And sometimes, Elston would help out by rubbing the ball against his shin guards and putting a nice big gouge in it, things like that. But this time, I gave it the old saliva treatment myself and then I threw Willie the biggest spitball you ever saw.

It started out almost at his chest and then it just broke down to the left, like dying when it got to the plate and dropping straight down without any spin. Willie just leaned into it a little and then stared at the ball while it snapped the hell out of sight, and the umpire shot up his right hand for strike three.

Okay, so I struck out Willie Mays. But to this day, people are probably still wondering why Mickey came running in from center field now that the inning was over, clapping his hands over his head and jumping up in the air like we'd just won the World Series—and here it was only the end of the first inning in the All-Star game, and he was going crazy all the way into the dugout. It was a money pitch, that's why, and we'd just saved ourselves four hundred dollars.

WILLIE MAYS:

At the time, I didn't know what was happening out there. I knew about Whitey's curve ball and his slider, but I didn't think he had a drop, too. I saw Mantle come in clapping his hands and acting sort of strange, and I couldn't believe it was only because they got me out in an All-Star game.

Later, they told me about it and why they loaded one up on me. Did they apologize for it? You must be kidding.

I'll tell you what impressed me about them over the years, though. They always could hurt you, whether Whitey was loading one up or not. They could beat you a lot of ways. People forget that besides all that power both ways, Mickey could fly. He'd go to first base from the left side of the plate in 3.1 seconds, or 3.2, and I never saw anybody do it that fast, not till Vada Pinson came in the league, anyway.

The big thing was his switch-hitting, though. You have a lot of switch-hitters who can hit the ball one way better than the other. But Mantle would hit it out either left-handed or right-handed on you. It meant you couldn't defense him. He just hit it, either way.

MICKEY:

I don't know what it was with us and All-Star games—maybe it was because we'd get three days off in the middle of the season and we'd get the chance to run around with some guys from the other clubs for a change—but I always looked forward to the All-Star game just to be with Don Drysdale the night before.

Like there was this time the game was in Washington, and me and Drysdale and Harvey Kuenn and Sandy Koufax and Whitey and I don't know, there were six or seven of us who got together the night before. We got into a cab at our hotel and told the driver to take us to the Gaslight Club, and he just made a big fat U-turn out the driveway and pulled up at the Gaslight Club—right across the street from the hotel we were staying in. I think he charged us a dollar apiece just to go across the street. One of our smart investments.

Anyway, later on that night, it was getting real light out by then and we were all at some after-hours spot, me and Drysdale and Kuenn and Whitey—I think the rest of the guys had gone home to get some sleep for the ball game. Anyway, we were sitting there drinking and a guy came in saying he was Harvey Kuenn, the baseball player, and giving us all this stuff about himself but not knowing Harvey Kuenn's sitting there with us drinking. Kuenn was funny, he listened to all this and let the guy hang himself all out and then told him who he was.

Finally, me and Drysdale were still wide awake so we went from the after-hours place to one of our suites in the hotel for a few more drinks, you know. And by now we're both looking pretty bad and we're starting to wonder about the Goddamned ball game that day. Drysdale, you know, besides being one of the best pitchers that I played against was probably the toughest right-handed pitcher I had to bat against, because he was so mean. It wasn't that he'd hurt you on purpose, but he had this big sidearm delivery and he was big and strong and he'd come whipping the ball at you from way the hell out in left field somewheres.

Like in spring training before an exhibition game, I'd be standing by the batting cage and he'd come walking past and he'd pat me on the ass and say, "Where'd you like to get it today, Mick?" And I knew he wasn't kidding, because he thought it was sort of funny to hit you in the ass. He didn't want you forgetting that he could be mean out there.

So this time, feeling and looking so bad after all that drinking, I figured that I'd better not take any chances—the way we figured in San Francisco that time with Willie Mays. I asked Drysdale, "Are you starting the game today?" And he said, yeah, and he got the idea that maybe we weren't in any shape by then for fighting each other too hard in the game. So he said, "I'll tell you what I'll do. I'll throw everything outside to you if you'll promise to swing at it." And I said, "You got a deal," because I didn't want the son of a bitch hitting me with that sidearm rocket of his. And we figured if we was drinking all night together, we might as well enjoy our hangover together all afternoon, and we did. At least I didn't have to worry about him killing me with that hard one, and he didn't have to worry about me getting hold of one off him.

We had some great times together, at All-Star games or golf tournaments, me and Drysdale and Billy Martin. One year, I remember it was at the baseball players' golf tournament down in Miami in spring training, and me and Billy rented one of those little convertible Thunderbirds. We used to load it up with ball players all the time, and we'd go around Miami Springs barhopping, and one night we were driving kind of fast or something. Billy's a pretty wild driver, especially if he's had a couple of drinks, and I think somebody must've called the police and said some guys in a red Thunderbird were running the lights or driving through town too fast.

Anyway, we didn't know they were looking for us, so we pulled into a place, an after-hours spot in Miami Villas, and went in to have another drink. Bobby Morgan and Drysdale and a bunch of the other players from the golf tournament were already in there drinking, and after a while Bobby Morgan wanted to know if he could use our car. So we said sure, it was parked right outside the bar. Billy had parked it right on the sidewalk.

We didn't know it, but meanwhile the police had finally found the car they were looking for, and they were sitting there waiting for somebody to come out and get in it. So who comes out but Bobby Morgan. He got in the little Thunderbird and started to give it the gas, but just as soon as he took off in it, there was police cars all around him with their red lights flashing. And they grabbed him and arrested him, and we were still inside the bar sitting around and drinking, and poor Morgan didn't know what the hell was going on.

WHITEY:

Remember the baseball players' golf tournament they had later that year down in Palm Springs, California? We were there with our wives, and Drysdale, Koufax and quite a few other guys. This was in October after the baseball season was over, and I think on the night of October 20 they brought in a little birthday cake for Mickey and me because Mickey's birthday is October 20 and mine is October 21.

I say "little" because it was gigantic: It must've been two feet in diameter and it was covered with whipped cream and was one of the biggest, gooiest cakes you ever saw. Jimmy Piersall was there, and he came over grabbing whipped cream off the cake with his fingers, and pretty soon he had cream all over his hands. Gene Freese was there, too. He played in the 1961 World Series for Cincinnati against us, and he and Piersall started kidding around with each other, flicking whipped cream and bothering each other. And the next thing you know, Piersall picked up the cake and let Freese have the whole thing right in his face.

The place just went crazy, there might've been around a hundred people there at the party. Freese was covered with this whipped cream from his head right on down to his toes. They had big glass windows in the room and outside there was a swimming pool with a little diving board, and through the windows the next thing we saw was Gene Freese getting up on the diving board and doing a perfect one-and-a-half into the pool with all his clothes on. Then he came back, as big as life, and spent the rest of the night at our birthday party, dripping wet in his suit.

The party didn't end there, though. After that, we met a good friend of Mickey's, a guy named Cecil Simmons, who was in charge of the gambling up at Wilbur Clark's Desert Inn at Las Vegas. He talked Mickey and me and Joan and Merlyn into going up there to spend a few days, and he even chartered an airplane that seated about eight people. So on the flight from Palm Springs to Vegas, he kept saying that he was going to have Betty pick us up at the airport, and we didn't know who the hell Betty was, but he kept talking about Betty all the way there.

Finally, we landed at Las Vegas and this beautiful blonde came walking up and gave Cecil a kiss, and who was it but Betty Grable. That's right. Since we were kids, she was our idol, Mickey's and mine, and I guess every other kid in the country who ever went to the movies. It just so happened that Cecil Simmons and his wife lived in the house next to Betty Grable and Harry James, right there alongside the fourth hole at the golf course of the Desert Inn. You won't believe this— we didn't believe it, either—but she not only drove us to the hotel but a night or two later she even cooked dinner for us in her home.

After dinner, we went back to the hotel and watched Harry James and his band at the Desert Inn. This was after the World Series and everything, and we'd been the center of attention on national TV and all the newspaper headlines, but even Joan and Merlyn were impressed with this: Betty Grable meeting us at the airport and cooking chicken for us in her own kitchen. Hell, I remember when I was twelve years old going to the movies and watching June Haver and Betty Grable in lots of pictures, and I always remember seeing that first pin-up picture of her during the war. We even used to go see Harry James at the Paramount. But I better go easy on that kind of "remembering"—it sounds like one ball player saying to another to needle him, "When I was a kid, you were always my hero," and the other guy usually replies by saying, "Go screw yourself."

We hung around Vegas a few nights after that and, as I said, Cecil Simmons sort of ran the gambling part of the business at the Desert Inn. So one night real late, the casino was just about empty and Mickey and I made one of our famous deals. We decided we'd get our wives drunk, then let them go on to bed and after that we could go bouncing around town to all the different places, just having a night out by ourselves, you know.

So we stuck around the bar for a long while and pretty soon Merlyn, who doesn't drink that much, had a couple of screwdrivers and decided she was going to bed. Okay. So now we're still stuck with Joan. She doesn't drink that much, either, but she can hold it pretty good if it's turning into a long night. Mickey and I kept trying to get a lot of drinks into her so she'd quit, too, and I guess we started around ten o'clock that evening. At four in the morning we were still in the bar; Mickey and I are just about passed out and Joan is still cold sober.

Finally, though, Joan gets up and says, "Well, I think I'll go to bed, boys," and off she goes. But by this time, there's no way we can go bouncing around—not in the shape we're in. So we decided to stick there and all, and so I said to Mickey, since there wasn't anything else left to do, "Give me fifty dollars." He was so loaded and so worn down by now that he just threw me fifty bucks, and I went over to the roulette table and I started betting on one color. Then I went back to the bar and announced, "We're out a hundred, give me another fifty."

So I took his fifty and my fifty and went over to the dice table and bet on one number over seven, and then in another thirty seconds we're out another hundred bucks. That's a hundred each so far, and Mickey was in worse shape than me, because he was still sitting there drinking while I was fruiting away our dough. So he said to me, "You give me fifty now." And, no kidding, he went over to the tables, came back in fifteen minutes and put twelve hundred dollars on the bar and said, "That's how to gamble."

So now we both get up and take the twelve hundred and head for the blackjack table. We really didn't know a hell of a lot about gambling; we were really ripe for a fall. But we had an angel this time. Cecil Simmons was still around, and he saw us drinking and playing, and he didn't want us to lose any of our money in his place. So he stood behind the dealer while Mickey was playing for us and I was standing next to him just watching him with our twelve hundred bucks.

Maybe Mickey would have a nineteen in his hand, you know, and he'd be standing pat. But Cecil would be looking over at the dealer's cards and if they'd say twenty, he'd say: "Hit him." And he kept that up till he was sure we weren't going to blow the twelve hundred that Mickey'd won for us.

I wound up being impressed as hell with a guy like Cecil Simmons, who looked after us when we didn't know any better. Mickey wound up being impressed with my wife. He said anybody who could drink like that must be some kind of freak.

You've got the idea by now that we weren't above a little finagling, like loading one up on Willie Mays, or making a deal with Drysdale not to hit Mickey in the behind with his fast ball. Once we even tried to rig a golf tournament. You know, one of those ball players' tournaments we were always getting into down in Miami. I think the City of Miami ran it in spring training as part of the tourist attraction. One time we figured we had a hell of a shot at one of our guys winning the whole thing. That was when the Yankees got Darrell Johnson, who'd played a lot of golf out in California. He was really red hot on the course, you know, he could shoot a 72. So we got all steamed up with the idea that he should get in this tournament right away and win it. You know, *we* weren't about to win it, so it might as well be Darrell.

I'm not sure we went about it the right way, though. Mickey and I would take him out every night and talk it up, trying to pump him up and get him as excited about it as we were. He was more like a pro, a lot cooler, sort of letting it happen, you know. He'd shoot a 72 maybe, and then a 71, and then we'd keep him out till all hours telling him what a hell of a job he was doing. Then the next day he'd go out and shoot an 83. Christ, by then you'd think Johnson would know that you can't mix golf with liquor, wouldn't you?

Looking back on it, though, I guess you can't ever get away from what you are, no matter whether you spend your time horsing around Las Vegas or Palm Springs or Miami, whether you're playing baseball or golf or just drinking with Toots Shor or Horace Stoneham or whoever.

In Kansas City once, Mickey and I and two of his friends from Dallas went out and played some golf. We got to this hole, and I was supposed to hit first. But I didn't know the course or anything, and Mickey did, so I said to him, "Where do you hit it here?" He said, "It's a dog-leg to the right. Just aim at that willow tree and you'll be okay.''

So I teed up and addressed the ball, and then I keep looking back and forth, down at the ball, then down the fairway, then at the ball again and then out on the course again. Finally, Mickey got pissed off waiting for something to happen and he hollered, ''God damn it, when you going to hit the ball?''

He should've known better, I suppose, because he's always kidding me about being a city slicker, and that time I guess East Sixty-sixth Street caught up with me. I turned around sort of embarrassed and said to him, ''What in hell does a willow tree look like?''

CONFESSIONS

WHITEY: **M**aybe I'm getting soft or mellow or something in my old age, but now that that story is out about how I loaded one up on Willie Mays, I might as well describe a few other cases. "Tricks" might be a better word. "Dirty tricks" sounds a little strong. Whatever you'd call them, I pitched in 498 games in the big leagues and I faced around 10,000 batters—10,000 guys I had to get out. And a few times, mostly late in my career when I could use a little help, I trotted out a few tricks to get me past the rough spots.

This doesn't involve Mantle, because there's not much a guy can do with a bat or glove to get an edge. Not the way a pitcher can. Every play in baseball begins with somebody putting the ball into play, and that somebody is the pitcher.

To start, let's go back to opening day in 1961 when I pitched against the Detroit Tigers. It was a real cold day, and cold weather can be a real problem for a pitcher. You can't get a good grip on the ball, it's that simple. The year before this opening day, I'd tried a few things to improve my grip on the ball, and this time I kind of perfected it.

What I did was to make a sticky stuff from a few well-selected ingredients. I took some turpentine, some baby oil, and some resin, and mixed them all together in a jar. It turned out like Elmer's glue. It was white stuff, not black, so you couldn't spot it on my fingers. I'd put it on both hands, on my uniform shirt, on as many places as I could, and I'd do it between innings in the dugout when nobody was watching me—least of all, the other club and the umpires.

Anyway, on this opening day in Detroit, I was ready with my magic elixir because it's always cold in April when the season begins. I even found a sophisticated way to keep the stuff stashed away: I bought a roll-on deodorant, took out the roll-on ball, emptied out the deodorant stuff, poured my sticky stuff in, and shoved the little can in the pocket of my warm-up jacket. Between innings, I'd just ooze some of it out onto my hands and fingers, and now I was getting a good grip on the ball, cold weather or no cold weather. We won the game all right, and then we all headed into the clubhouse. The only fly in the ointment, so to speak, was our old friend Yogi Berra.

The thing was that Yogi was always borrowing everybody's stuff, their after-shave lotion or shaving cream or hair tonic. He'd be on his way to the shower room and he'd just reach into your locker and help himself to a dash of whatever he needed. Nobody minded too much, even though the guys would pretend to run him off.

Well, leave it to Mantle to put two and two together. Mickey always knew what I was up to; we didn't have any secrets from each other. He knew that Yog was always mooching stuff from guys' lockers, so after this game with the Tigers, he went and put my sticky stuff on the shelf in my locker—where Yogi would be sure to see it.

Sure enough, Yogi came out of his own locker and saw this deodorant can on my shelf and helped himself. All the writers were still crowded around me because I'd just won the opener, but the next thing we heard was Yogi hollering and bellowing things like "Son of a bitch, what the hell is this stuff?" And he was off to the side there cursing and writhing around—no kidding, his arms were stuck to his sides.

Mickey and I were the only guys on the club who knew what it was and, with the writers hanging around trying to interview me, we didn't want to give it away. So we got Yogi into the trainer's room inside, and the trainer had to use alcohol to dissolve all that stuff, and finally he had to cut the hair under Yog's arms to release him. Boy, was he boiling. But I was afraid that he might spill the beans on my sticky stuff. I can imagine how it must've hurt him to get all stuck together like that. But that was his tough luck; I still didn't want him giving away my thing.

Look, they didn't call me "Slick" for nothing, but I wasn't the only pitcher in baseball who gave himself a little edge. The other clubs were always watching me like hawks, but some guys made a living by doing tricks with balls. You could put greasy stuff anywhere on your uniform or body and then touch it during the game. I remember the time they made Pete Ramos change his shirt three times in a game in Baltimore. The umpire kept sending him back inside to put on a clean shirt because the Orioles were yelling that he was throwing a wet one. And maybe Ramos was. That "Cuban palm ball" of his did a lot of tricks coming up to the plate.

Some guys would put greasy stuff in places like the tongue of their shoe—you were always reaching down and fixing your shoe in a game. But you had to be careful there because you were loading it up in full view of everybody. When Johnny Keane became manager of the Yankees after leaving the Cardinals, he told me once that some guys in St. Louis used to put a hunk of stuff on the sleeve of their sweatshirt. Then they'd rub their fingers there during the game and get some grease on the ball, and let it fly.

Eddie Lopat and I used pine tar a few times, but it was black and it would cake on your fingers. Between innings you'd have to wash it off with alcohol. Not so good. But Lopat was a master. He'd even make a project out of it, like a science student in college. When he and I were in the trainer's room, he'd mix the stuff up. You remember that when I first joined the Yankees, Lopat would coach me about how to pitch to every batter in the league. He was like my tutor, and I guess this became part of my education.

It's funny, when people get the idea that you're liable to cheat a little, they always get on you, whether you're doing it or not. Sometimes that works in your favor: If they *think* you're loading the ball somehow, you've got them at a psychological disadvantage, thinking the ball's going to do tricks. Even when I wasn't fooling around—like when I was warming my fingers on a hot-water bottle or something—guys like Charlie Dressen would be screaming to the umpires about me, anyway.

Now that I think about it, the only Yankees who used to get protests were Ramos and me. Pedro was a fine pitcher and I used to spend a lot of time with him, but he never told me what he did to the ball. His "code," I guess. So once I figured I'd give him a dose of his own medicine.

Pete thought he was a pretty good hitter, and he actually was a good hitter for a pitcher. He'd hit home runs sometimes and, when we opened the Astrodome in an exhibition game against the Houston club, he was out there before the game trying to hit a ball off the ceiling, which was a couple of hundred feet high. This other time in spring training, I said to him: "I've got a pitch you can't hit, no matter what you do." And he grabs a bat right away, and he's going to waffle it.

So I loaded up the ball with mud. I put some mud on one side of it, the idea is to keep the mud spot on top of the ball and then throw it like a fast ball. The mud will stay in the same position for a while, and then the weight of the mud and the resistance it gives the air will finally force the ball to drop like a screwball. It's the same as if you cut the ball, keep the cut on top, and fire it like the fast ball. It'll drop like hell. I still show it to young pitchers sometimes in spring training.

Actually, I only used the "mud ball" or the "cut ball" in

my last couple of years with the Yankees—you know, to stick around the big leagues a little longer. I'd spit in my right hand with the glove off, then I'd pretend to be wiping it off. But I wouldn't wipe it off. I'd be rubbing and wiping but I'd keep missing the wet spot on my right hand. Then I'd bend over and reach for the resin bag and scuff it in the dirt. You had to be careful they didn't catch you doing it. So maybe the first five times, I'd have the ball in my glove when I reached for the resin bag with my bare hand. But the sixth time, I'd have it in my bare hand and I'd get resin and dirt and some spit on the ball all at once, and they'd never catch on.

So much for technique. Anyway, when I tried it on Pedro Ramos that day in spring training, the ball came up to him like a fast one and he'd swing for the fences. He never touched it. Pete was sure I was loading it, but he didn't know how. I told him it was *my* Cuban palm ball.

Timing is important when you're working with tricks. Sometimes I wouldn't use a loaded pitch at all in a game, whether it was a mud ball or a cut ball or a sticky ball. Sometimes I'd throw it to get a strikeout—or a ground ball. You could usually get a ground ball because the pitch was sinking, and a ground ball could get you out of an inning.

I remember in 1968 when I wasn't pitching any more, I was a coach then and we were playing the Mets in the annual exhibition, the Mayor's Trophy Game. Ralph Houk was running the club again, and he said to me, "You want to have some fun? Pitch one inning tonight."

I was in the bullpen warming up for my inning and I rubbed hell out of the ball in the cement. Got it all good and ripped up. Mickey was playing first base for us, so I got on the bullpen phone between innings and called the dugout and told him to use the game ball for infield practice before the next inning. You know, instead of using an old beat-up brown ball to throw grounders to the infielders, pick up the game ball that the other pitcher dropped on the grass and pretend it was the infield ball. So Mickey did it, and the umpires didn't notice.

Now I come in from the bullpen hiding my scuffed-up baseball in my glove, and the Mets never came close to it. I fanned Ed Charles on three pitches, got Tommie Agee on three, and then Ed Kranepool grounded out weakly. It would take a pitcher to suspect something right away—like it takes a thief to catch one—and so Dick Selma came running over from the Mets' dugout demanding to inspect the ball. I just laughed and walked off the mound. But after the game, Selma came over again holding my bullpen ball in his hand— all cut and almost bleeding, it was cut so bad—and asked me to autograph it for him. Like Willie Sutton autographing a bank vault.

That was only an exhibition game but, since I'm making a kind of confession here, I'll admit that I went to the other extreme once and loaded a few in a World Series. Not that it did me or the Yankees any good. We still got shallumped by the Dodgers, four straight, in 1963. But I tried.

It was the fourth game, me against Sandy Koufax, and Koufax already had set a record by striking out fifteen of our guys in the first game. Now we were in L.A., and they only needed one more game to wrap up the Series. Like I say, I tried. I threw mostly mud balls or cut balls the whole game. You would have to say I had pretty good luck, too, because the Dodgers only got two hits off me. One was a single by big Frank Howard in the second inning. The other—well, Howard again, in the fifth. He was big and strong, like a friendly monster, and I guess I didn't cut the ball enough. Frank whacked it into the upper deck in left field, farther than anybody else had ever hit one in Dodger Stadium. Later, they even painted the seat a different color, as though it was some kind of landmark.

Mickey hit one off Koufax that traveled just about as far. But the Dodgers still won the game, 2 to 1, after Joe Pepitone lost one of Clete Boyer's throws in the background of shirts and the sun. I used enough mud that day to build a dam, but not enough to hold back the Dodgers.

I haven't said much about spitballs because, outside of that one I fed to Willie in the All-Star game, I can remember throwing only one other in my whole career. But I remember that one pretty clearly. We were playing Kansas City and the batter was Manny Jiminez, a pretty good hitter with power. I used to try throwing a spitter on the sidelines but couldn't control it, which is probably why I didn't go to it in games. But this time, we had a big lead anyway, so I decided to give it a whirl. Boy, it dropped about a foot, he missed it by that much for strike three, and Elston was lucky even to stop it.

That was 1964 when I was struggling a bit. They always thought I used it, I know that. But I really couldn't control it, so I didn't—except that one time. No kidding, my first year with the club, Joe Page tried to show me how to throw a wet one, although I doubt he used it in a game. He just reared back and fired. That's what you do when you're young and strong. That's what Pete Ramos did. He was only nineteen when he came up, and he could throw fast as hell. It was only toward the end, when he became a relief pitcher, that he started heaving the spitter.

Let me put it this way: When I was young, it was a bigger thing for me to throw a curve ball on 2 and 0, not a spitter. The tricks came later.

Funny, it never bothered Mickey, what we're talking about. I never heard him complain that the pitcher was throwing him a spitball. Never heard him bitch that guys were cheating. He used to wear out guys like Ramos, anyway. And maybe he didn't want to embarrass me.

What he'd really complain about was low sliders around his ankles by guys like Jim Bunning or Bob Shaw. He thought they were throwing at him that way. Not at his head, at his bad legs. Even if they didn't hit him, it was painful for him to jump out of the way. Once, after Bunning made him scatter, he said, "If that guy throws once more at my ankles,

I'm going out there and kick the shit out of him.''

The Yankees were a tough team to get cute with. We could beat Bunning—we'd crowd the lineup with those left-handed hitters, because he was a righty, and he didn't have much chance. It took a guy like Frank Lary of the Tigers to beat us consistently. Don't ask me why, he just did, even though he was right-handed, too. In that little park in Detroit we could send up all those left-handed power hitters like Mantle, Maris, Kubek, Pepitone and Berra. But we'd still get one run off Lary, and they'd get two.

Getting back to the tricks, when the other guys were watching me so much, Elston sometimes would cut the ball on his shin guards for me. He figured he'd help me out by giving it a little nick before tossing it back to me. But it was hard for him to cut it good on the little metal rivet on his shin guard.

Okay, so much for the mud and the cuts and the spitters. They were child's play compared to the main event: the *Ring*. I always figured that'd be a secret forever, but since I'm laying it all on the line, I might as well go all the way.

The ring. I had this friend who was a jeweler, and I had him make up a ring for me. This was late in my career, and I was really using my street-smart overtime. I told him exactly what I wanted—a half-inch-by-quarter-inch piece of a rasp, all nice and scratchy like a file. Then we got this stainless steel ring and he welded it onto the hunk of rasp.

I'd wear the ring on my right hand like a wedding ring and, since I'm left-handed, that was my glove hand. So, during games, I'd just stand behind the mound like any other pitcher rubbing up a new ball and I'd take the glove off and rub up the ball. That rasp would do some job on it, too. Whenever I needed a ground ball, I'd cut it good. It was as though I had my own tool bench out there with me.

To hide it, I even got a skin-colored Band-Aid and wrapped it around the ring to match my finger. Camouflage and all.

I also worked out some signs with Elston to warn him which way the ball was going to break. I'd flap my glove, meaning that I was going to try something, the way pitchers flap their glove when they're recycling the catcher's signals or adding numbers to them. You know, like a quarterback calling an automatic at the line of scrimmage. But in my case, the flap told the catcher to keep his eyes open because I had something going. Then I'd brush my glove down or across my body to give him an extra clue what to expect.

I've got to admit it worked like a charm. Nobody got on to it, and I didn't go around talking about it in the dugout or anything like that—guys get traded to other teams, and I didn't want *that* to get around. Then one day we were playing Cleveland in Yankee Stadium and my ring and I pitched together for the last time. They caught me using it. They didn't realize exactly what was going on, but it was a close call, too close to keep tempting fate with.

I had just struck out a guy and Elston rolled the ball back to the mound because it was the third out in the inning. Then the Indians' pitcher, Mudcat Grant, came out to pitch and he picked up the ball. Right away he showed it to the umpire, who for some reason didn't say anything.

For a minute, I thought maybe I was getting a reprieve. But it didn't last. Alvin Dark, who was the Indians' manager, started saving foul balls that were hit into their dugout, and finally he showed them to the umpire, Hank Soar. And Soar came over to me and said, "How are you cutting the ball?"

Then he spotted my ring and got to the point. "What's that?" he asked me. And—Joannie forgive me—I said, "My wedding ring."

Well, all hell didn't break loose, as I thought it would. But they were on to me, so I slipped the old rasp-ring into my pants and got rid of it after the inning was over. I couldn't afford to be caught with the evidence on me.

After a game in those days, I used to give the ring to our trainer, Joe Soares, and he'd wrap it up in some gauze and hide it in the bottom of one of his trunks with the pills and bandages and medical supplies. The year after I quit pitching, I was going to show the ring to Steve Hamilton, one of our pitchers, who also was a professor down in Kentucky in the off-season. So I went to Joe and said, "Where's the ring?" He said, "I threw it out the day after you retired. I wasn't going to get caught with that thing in my medical case."

Imagine that. After all those delicate moves on the mound, Joe Soares chickened out. I guess I should've been happy that I'd never been caught, either. But I was sort of teed off.

"Hell," I said, kind of irritated, "it cost me a hundred bucks to have it made."

THE CANADIAN BOMB
SHELTER SURVIVAL COMPANY

The modern professional athlete has been portrayed as a man of distinction who comes lurching into your living room with briefcase, bonus, business manager, tax shelter, supersell, and Howard Cosell. Overpaid, underworked, glorified, commercialized, and he's got it made.

Until the 1960s, he enjoyed a certain "hero" status but in most cases didn't bring home enough investment money to strike it truly rich. A few old heroes, like Casey Stengel and Al Lopez, got into oil wells and got out wealthy. Others sold themselves to Wheaties and Gillette Blue Blades. Chuck Connors became The Rifleman on television, and Yogi Berra hit it with Yoo-Hoo, the chocolate drink. But most baseball players wound up on bubblegum cards that small boys bought cheap and traded fast.

Then, in the sixties, the gold rush was on. As the leagues grew and the talent wars raged, the agents and business managers arrived with deals and a whole new language: deferred income, pensions, tax shelters, endorsements, package plans, and capital gains. A man's paycheck provided his source money, his investments provided the nest egg.

By the seventies, no man worth his salt had failed to

"sign." Joe Namath, one of the pioneers of the stampede, signed with the New York Jets for $425,000 a year and with Fabergé cosmetics for $2,000,000 for eight years. Walt Frazier signed with the New York Knicks for $450,000 a year and became president of Walt Frazier Enterprises at a fortune more (investing *other* athletes' money). Catfish Hunter auctioned himself to the Yankees for $3,750,000 in salary, life insurance and fringe benefits, and then started to appear in commercials for trucks, farm equipment and dog food. Pelé, the soccer hero of Brazil, retired at thirty-four and unretired at thirty-four-plus-a-few-months when Warner Communications came through with a three-year contract: One hundred games a year and "promotional" work for a total take of $4,700,000.

It took money to make money, and yesterday's shortstop stood a good chance of becoming tomorrow's conglomerate, if he played his cards right. Or, if he had the real smarts, he might even score a coup like the one achieved by Dick Hall, a forty-year-old relief pitcher for the Baltimore Orioles whose stiff-legged and stiff-armed style once was compared somewhat unfavorably with that of "Molly Klutz." When he was done pitching for the Orioles in the World Series, Hall would hurry to his business office, hang out his shingle as a certified public accountant, and pitch in with his colleagues in auditing company books—including those of a client named the Baltimore Orioles. Not everybody was blessed with the Midas touch, though. Every once in a while, some pro athlete—some big pro athlete—would lunge onto the scene and the vultures would swoop down, certain that Barnum had called the shot: A sucker is born every minute, especially in the middle of a gold rush.

MICKEY:
There was always two things you could count on if you stayed with the Yankees long enough when they kept winning—and I don't mean booze and broads. Most ball clubs

could count on them even if they weren't winning all the time. I mean money and attention, and most of the time you got the attention because you'd already got the money.

Look, I started with the club at seventy-five hundred, and got it up to a hundred thousand, besides the fact that me and Whitey worked out that deal where they'd let us sign for everything in the hotels. And we figured out that from Whitey's first year with the team, which was 1950, up until the last year the Yankees won the pennant, which was in 1964, the ball club got into the World Series thirteen times and won it eight times. Counting the winner's and loser's shares, that meant something like a hundred thousand dollars right there in what they call prize money. And today, guys make even more.

On top of that, because the Yankees played in New York, we always used to get followed around and you might say even hounded because we had more newspaper writers and more television and radio than anywheres else. You couldn't scratch your ass without some guy trying to find out why. And remember, New York had four or five morning papers then and four or five different ones in the afternoon, and they all had reporters and columnists traveling around with the club, especially after the Dodgers and the Giants went to California. And Casey attracted attention like he was the star of a vaudeville show.

Then, with all that going for us, our guys always did some big things when the money was there and everybody was watching every move. You know, like Slick here won ten World Series games and Reynolds won seven, and Larsen pitched the perfect game. And we used to hit pretty good, too, like Johnny Mize hit three home runs in the 1952 Series, I think it was, and the same year Yogi and I got two each and Billy Martin and McDougald and Woodling got one each. We hit ten that time, and nine in the Series the next year. Me and Billy and McDougald got a couple apiece, and Yogi and Collins and Woodling got one. And one year, it must've been

'56 when Larsen pitched his no-hitter, me and Yogi hit three out each, and Billy got two for himself. And a couple years later, Bauer hit four and I got a couple, and in 1960, I got three.

Before we got done, I played in sixty-five games in the Series and got eighteen home runs. And Whitey started twenty-two times, which was a record for a pitcher, and he went thirty-three or thirty-four innings in a row without giving up a run, which broke a record that Babe Ruth set when he was pitching. So we never had a hell of a lot of privacy, with all that going on. The hell of it was, we didn't turn out too smart when we started drawing people who tried to get us to put our money in their businesses and schemes and things. We were what you might call real suckers.

One of my better business deals happened in 1956, I think it was, because I had a real good year and won the Triple Crown. Anyway, we were still living in Commerce at that time, we'd just built a house there, and one evening me and Merlyn were just getting ready to eat when a Cadillac pulled up to the house. You don't see many Cadillacs in Commerce. And a guy gets out of the car, he has on a great big cowboy suit and hat and a suede jacket, and cowboy boots, and he looks pretty rich. He comes up and knocks on the door and tells me his name is C. Roy Williams. He says he needs to talk to me about a way we can make a lot of money.

Says he was working on this *in*surance company, the Will Rogers Insurance Company. And he says that, you know, if you got in on the ground floor of New York Life or of Equitable ten years ago, look how much money you'd be making now.

So right away, Merlyn picked him out and she called me in the kitchen and said to me, "Look, this guy's a phoney, Mickey."

I told her, don't worry, I won't do anything with him. But of course, he showed us policies he'd had printed up, with caricatures of me and Merlyn. He showed us how he was going to have pictures of me and Merlyn walking down the street holding hands and then little Mickey holding her hand—that was going to be on the front of the policy. He had them all printed up before he came there. And he said that I could get into the thing for like five thousand dollars, and own half the company.

And me and Merlyn gave him a can of beer or something and got off in the other room and started talking again and she said, "Look, he's a phoney." And I said, "Look, I'll tell you what I'm going to do about it." Well, about this same time, we were starting the Micky Mantle Motel up in Joplin, Missouri, with Mr. Harold Youngman, the guy who was kind of like my adviser, and she said go up and talk to Harold about this here deal.

So I took the guy up there and got the guy to talk to Harold, and Harold, of course, asked the guy who his lawyers were and who he was connected with, things like that. Some background on him, you know. Bunch of things like that. So, just talking to him, Harold found out the guy was a shyster, his lawyer was some guy Harold knew. Harold's a construction man in Oklahoma, and he knows a lot of people there. He found out the guy's lawyer was a shyster from Pryor, Oklahoma, and the guy was actually a shyster and con artist himself.

He called me in and told me that, and on the way home the guy was talking to me and I said, I can't do this because Harold's my adviser, you know, and all this. And the guy says he's sorry because it was going to make a lot of money, and he was going down to see Jim Sholters and *he* was going to put five thousand dollars in the company, or maybe it was a couple of thousand. But on the way back to Commerce, he was telling me this, and he said to me, if you change your mind, we're staying at a motel between Commerce and Miami, Oklahoma, and it's only about two and a half or three miles. If you change you mind, let me know, I'll be staying all night, and we'll probably have room for you in the company yet. But if you wait too long, we'll be gone in the morning and there won't be any room for you to get in the Will Rogers Insurance Company. And he told me some other good things, like the insurance I'd be getting for just getting in on the ground floor of the company.

Anyway, when we got back to my house, there was another big Cadillac sitting there, and that was his wife, sitting out in front. Or, he said it was his wife. So we sit there a little while, and then I take him to his car and he leaves.

But all night long, I'm thinking about it—now what if Harold and Merlyn are wrong and this guy's on the up-and-up? What if I let this go by, and it goes into a multimillion-dollar company, and I lose out because I didn't give him five thousand dollars?

So I get up early the next morning, after thinking about it more and more. We'd just gotten our World Series checks, and I'd just put our Series check in the Bank of Commerce. We didn't have too much money then. We'd just built our house, so we probably had about ten thousand dollars in the bank. But anyway, I wrote out a check for five thousand and went over to the motel, getting all charged up and hoping he hadn't gone yet so I wouldn't miss out. He was still there, so I gave him the check and figured now I was the half-owner of the Will Rogers Insurance Company.

Maybe a week later, there's a knock on the door and a guy says he's from the F.B.I. He was looking for a guy that just got out of prison, and he asked if a guy had been bothering us. I said, yeah. And he said, well, I hope you didn't give him any money. And I said, I'm sorry, but I did.

It turns out they were looking for him, and he left a trail that went right through my house. So they kept on looking for him, but by the time they found him, he'd sold both cars and got rid of all the money. They put him back in jail. But from what they told me later, he'd been in jail thinking up this whole scheme, reading in the papers while he was in jail about the good year I'd had. And the year that Jim Sholters had. So he got out and headed straight for me. I don't know if he got the other guy, but he got this one, and it was one of the first sucker deals I ever made—and one of the biggest.

WHITEY:

When you put us together, the chances were twice as good that somebody might pick our pockets. At least, back in those days when we still didn't know our ass from a sound investment.

There was this guy named Ted Boomer—how's that for a name? And wait'll you hear what he was unloading on us. He got us up in the hotel in Cleveland one day and gave us a big long story about how we were going to make millions in this company called—are you ready?—the Canadian Bomb Shelter Survival Company. No fooling, the Canadian Bomb Shelter Survival Company. We were going to build bomb shelters in Canada.

I think Mickey and I put up about five thousand dollars each, and for that we got ten thousand shares of stock each. So after Ted Boomer tells us this, he says to me—after everybody leaves—that I should stay. Then, after they leave, he says he wants to put me on the board of directors, and "I am going to give you an extra twenty-five thousand shares for nothing." For nothing. So I couldn't wait to get down to the room and tell Mickey, because I was going to split it with him. After all, we shared everything, you know.

I rushed down to our room and said to him, now we have forty-five thousand shares of stock in the Goddamned thing —ten thousand apiece plus the extra twenty-five. And we were just a few years from East Sixty-sixth Street and from Spavinaw, Oklahoma.

Well, we met the guy once or twice after that, and everything was getting set up, he was telling us, and after that we were going to start making the bomb shelters in the United States and then start collecting on them when all the people got around to buying them. Finally, all of a sudden we got our stock certificates—and all of a sudden, we didn't see Ted Boomer any more. To this day, I don't have the slightest idea where the hell he is. And to this day, I still have the forty-five thousand shares of stock at home.

The Will Rogers Insurance Company and the Canadian Bomb Shelter Survival Company, my ass.

Now we've got a lot of things going, like all the commercials on TV. But probably the best investment we ever made was when Harold Youngman got us into the Holiday Inn down there in Joplin. Harold owned some property there just on the turnpike when you're going from St. Louis to Kansas City. I think it was Route 71, you have to go on this route to go from the Oklahoma Turnpike to another turnpike. Anyway, we started with thirty-five units and then we added some in the back a year later, and then a little while later we doubled that. I think when we sold them we had over a hundred units, and I think that I owned five or six percent of it.

I know I invested fifteen thousand over a period of ten years, and we like tripled our investment for what we put in. Mickey and I still get checks from that, and it's probably the best investment we ever made.

But I guess the happiest time I ever had putting my money in something was with horses. I was a city kid and didn't know too much about horses at first, but after I met Delvin Miller, it all changed. You know, Del Miller, who breeds and raises trotters out in western Pennsylvania and drives them all over the world. He's in the harness racing Hall of Fame. He's made plenty of money in horses and he's one of the greatest characters we ever ran into.

The first time we met Del Miller was when Mickey was running a little golf tournament in Mount Plymouth, Florida, outside Orlando. The money was going to Hodgkin's disease, to the foundation, because Mickey's father died from the disease. We got a few name guys like Cary Middlecoff the golfer and Birdie Tebbetts the baseball manager to come and play. And somebody invited Billy Haughton, who's one of the top guys in the harness-racing business, and Del Miller, though we didn't know them then. It was forty-five degrees that day and forty-mile-an-hour winds were blowing, and maybe a hundred people showed up for the golf tournament. So it wasn't exactly a financial success. But we did get to meet Billy and Del.

A few years later, Del got me interested in horses—I even learned to train horses for him after a while. He got me to invest in them, too, and the best one I ever had was a horse I sold in 1974 called Spitfire Hanover. We bought the horse a few years earlier as a baby; Del paid $3,900 for him. Then Arnold Palmer, who doesn't live too far from Del out in Pennsylvania, called and asked if I'd mind letting him in, too. I said sure, and Arnie sent us a check for $1,300 for his one-third share.

Spitfire Hanover won over forty thousand dollars in 1973 as a two-year-old and about sixty thousand dollars up until August in 1974. Then a gentleman from Italy bought him from us for one-hundred-eighty thousand dollars. Our accountant figured out that Arnie, for his one thousand three hundred dollars share, made over eighty thousand dollars profit. Del drove Spitfire in the Hambletonian and then won a big race at Roosevelt Raceway.

Delvin has this big farm—maybe four hundred or five hundred acres—in Meadowlands, not very far from Pittsburgh. He used to keep Adios there; you know, Adios, who was the greatest sire of all time. He died about five or six years ago when he was twenty-five, and all the greatest pacers are related to him now. Del and I had a mare that we bred every year, she was named Meadow Ford after me, and the next one was called Meadow Mickey, after you-know-who. Del was offered twenty-five thousand dollars for him, and I said we better take it. Del said the horse probably could run about as fast as Mantle but that he probably had bad knees, too.

Mickey never did get any horses with us, but in 1973 Del talked Mickey and me into racing at his track, the Meadows, out there in his hometown. He talked me and Mickey into putting on this match before the main race, just the two of us. It was a match race before the big Adios race, which is for a hundred thousand dollars.

So when we were still in Florida, he said, "You better learn how to drive a horse before you try racing one." Well, I'd been driving for years by then because this was a long time after we first met Delvin, and I'd been training horses, so I knew what I was doing. But Mickey had never been on one—maybe just on a mule back home. So we go out to the track early in the morning so Del can show him how to drive a harness horse, and Del fixes the three of us up with three horses the first morning. Del says to Mickey, "Stay on the inside on the rail and in front of us. I'll stay on the outside and Whitey, you stay in back of Mickey." And that's the way we drive around the mile.

So toward the end of the mile, going around the last turn into the stretch, Del looks back and winks at me over his shoulder, sort of motioning that he's going to pull something. Like something to scare Mickey. What he does is start steering his horse in towards Mickey's horse on the rail. Mickey starts getting a little nervous now. At the same time that Del's crowding him into the rail, I bring my horse up and put his head right the hell on Mickey's shoulder, and by this time my horse is snorting and the saliva is coming out of his mouth all over Mickey's shoulder. We had Mickey boxed in. He was scared silly because he didn't know what the hell was going on. He figured he'd either get knocked into the rail by Delvin's horse or bitten on the shoulder by mine.

Well, we kept practicing for a few days down there, and

then a few months later we had the race up at Meadowlands. Son of a bitch if Mickey didn't beat me. How's that for beginner's luck? Then a month or so later, the people at Vernon Downs asked if we'd come up there and have another match race. They'd give us a little fee, like the jockeys get, and some expense money, and they had one of the biggest weekday crowds in their history that night. We wore Del Miller's silks, brown and yellow, and they tried to pick horses for us that were pretty even—and Mantle beat me again.

Now these were the only two times he'd ever raced, and he was 2 for 2 against me. But we finally had a third match race down at the Pompano track near Fort Lauderdale in the spring of 1974 when we were coaching for the Yankees. They gave Mickey a real bad horse, I'm happy to say. I even had trouble slowing mine down enough to make it look like a real close race. Sure enough, the next morning we found that Mickey's horse had broken a bone in his foot during the race. Even though he could finish the race, I saw when I was passing him on the turn that he wasn't striding right. I was trying to keep my horse going as slow as I could, but I still beat him by six or seven lengths.

Mickey is still screaming about that one—how they gave him a horse with a broken foot and that's the only time I could beat him.

DEL MILLER:
The way it happened was that Whitey and I were talking about driving harness horses that day at the golf tournament in Orlando, and Whitey said, "I'd like to try that." Then when Mickey heard that, he said to Whitey, "Hell, I can beat you driving those horses." And for about the next ten years, he kept challenging Whitey—on golf courses, in bars, everywhere. I asked him, "You ever drive?" And he said, "Only mules back in Missouri."

He did show talent for it, I thought. But Whitey kept putting him off, and, I think, pissing him off. But finally he agreed to race Mickey. I was a little afraid they might hurt each other, so I made damn sure they were schooled and ready for it. It would've been bad publicity if they got hurt.

Well, as you know, Mickey won two out of three races from Whitey. But I suppose if you'd given them evenly matched horses, it would've been a photo finish each time. When Whitey finally beat him in that third match down at Pompano, right away Mickey started accusing me of stacking it against him so's Whitey could win. But I wouldn't do that to a friend. Hell, they even tossed a coin to see who'd get which horse. If you *do* think I'd stack it just to raise a little hell, you might be right, at that. They were always out trying to screw each other up in little rivalries, whether it was drinking a certain whiskey or driving a certain horse. I remember one day we were playing golf at Boca Raton; there were four of us, myself and Whitey and Mickey and Phil Rizzuto. And Whitey hit a ball that landed way out in the rough on the muddy ground alongside a creek.

Well, he couldn't play it, so he elected to "drop" one— you know, drop the ball over his shoulder and take a penalty stroke and then play it from wherever it landed that time. So he turned around and dropped the ball over his shoulder just as I happened to be passing behind him, coming over to see what in hell was going on. I was just passing behind him when he dropped the ball and I caught it in the air and just kept walking away with the ball.

Whitey turned around to line up his shot, but now he couldn't find the ball anywhere. He searched around for a while, then said, "Goddamn, I must've dropped it in the water. I guess it rolled in the creek." By then, Mickey and Rizzuto were "helping" him hunt for it, and so was I. Were we good sports about it? You bet we were. We let him drop another ball and take a penalty on a penalty.

WHITEY:

Yeah, we were like brothers, all right—like Frank and Jesse James. But we couldn't have had a better partner in the horse business than Delvin. He has this tremendous farm we've been to many times, and in back of the main house he's got this tremendous brick barn and two silos that go up where they store grain or wheat or something. They hadn't been using them for years, so Del took the one silo, a nice big round one about thirty feet across, and made an apartment out of it. It's the most beautiful thing I've ever seen, or stayed in, or drank in.

In 1973, when Mickey and I had the first race, he and I and Eddie Arcaro stayed there a few nights—in the silo, about a hundred yards behind the house. I'll never forget Eddie Arcaro because when he came there he'd just had open-heart surgery. You know, here's a guy who won the Kentucky Derby five times, and he just had open-heart surgery. So I said, "How do you feel, Eddie?" And he said, "The doctor says I'll be fine as long as I don't drink, smoke, or stay up late at night."

So for the three nights we stayed there, I don't think I ever saw a drink or a smoke out of Eddie's hand. I think we averaged maybe one hour's sleep for each of the three nights we stayed there, and he was still going strong.

In the evening, we'd walk over to Del's house where he had this big open porch where anybody might show up. Everybody was invited, and they just came there. You were liable to see Arnold Palmer there one night, or Freddie van Lennep, who owns Castleton Farms down in Kentucky and is one of the biggest horse breeders in the country. Or Helen Boehm, whose husband was the sculptor who made the famous "Boehm Birds." She got into the horse business herself, and she travels to Europe with Del and his wife, Mary Lib. Her husband made this replica of Adios, and I think it's presented every year to the winner of the Adios Pace. Or maybe Perry Como would come over and sit on the back porch with us one night, and sing.

Some of the old Yankees used to show up, too: guys like George Selkirk and Charlie Keller. Keller got deep into breeding and racing horses when he and Joe DiMaggio were batting 3 and 4 in the lineup in the thirties and forties. Keller's got this big farm down in Maryland—they used to call him "King Kong" and "the Maryland strong boy" because he really had frightening muscles. The very first horse I bought was one that Charlie had bred; I bought it at the sale down in Harrisburg seven or eight years ago. It was called Yankee Mac, and I paid eight thousand dollars for him. But right after we got the horse back to Roosevelt Raceway, he was kicking in his stall and he kicked the cement wall and chipped a sesamoid bone, and was never really any good after that. Charlie felt just terrible because the horse had a pretty good chance to turn out sharp, but not after the accident.

Keller comes down to Florida every spring and spends a month with Del Miller, and we all play a lot of golf, since Mickey and I are usually at the Yankees' camp then, anyway. Talk about wearing the word "Yankee" on your T-shirt, Keller names almost all his horses Yankee something-or-other, like Yankee Mac, my first horse; or Yankee Bambino, who won the first heat at the Hambletonian in 1975 and who was named for Babe Ruth; and there was Fresh Yankee, this famous mare that won over a million dollars after Charlie sold her for something like nine hundred dollars. No, Fresh Yankee wasn't named for me.

Then there was the day our interest in horses nearly went on the rocks, along with a lot of our other interests like life insurance and bomb shelters. You remember Round Table, the great race horse? He ran in the Kentucky Derby in 1957, the year we lost the Series to Milwaukee in seven games. We were playing in Chicago that summer and Marge Everett Lindheimer, who owned the track there—or at least her father did then—invited me and Mickey and Casey out to the races with her. We were her guests and had a big time, we had lunch with her upstairs at the track and we watched the races and all.

Then the public relations man for the track asked us if we'd like to take a picture with Round Table, who had run an exhibition race that day. We said okay, even though Mickey wasn't too fond of horses at that time.

Anyway, we went down to the track where they had Round Table, and he'd just run seven furlongs and he was still a little excited. So now both Mickey and the horse are a little jittery. But they grouped us around the horse and were posing us for the picture and, sure enough, just as they were snapping it, Round Table got upset and stepped right on Mickey's foot. Casey and I were pretty worried that maybe Mickey couldn't play that day, and I guess Marge Lindheimer was worried that Round-Table might've got hurt and couldn't run. I could just see the headlines on that one.

MICKEY:
Yeah, "Round Table Steps on Mantle's Foot." I could just see old C. Roy Williams reading that in his newspaper back in his jail cell. And me the half-owner of the Will Rogers Insurance Company.

CHANGING THE GUARD

It happened in threes. Phase I started in 1949, ended in 1953, and included five straight pennants and world championships. And no baseball team in history matched that run of success—including, as it turned out, the Yankees themselves in Phases II and III.

There was a pause in 1954 while the New York Giants and Cleveland Indians replaced them in center stage. Then they launched the middle years, like the Russians launching another five-year plan, though with a few cracks in the facade. For example, in 1955 they won the pennant again but this time lost the World Series to Brooklyn, and it was the first time they had lost one in twenty-three years. Then they regained the full touch in 1956, took the pennant by nine games over Cleveland and watched Mantle lead the league in total offense: batting .358, hitting 52 home runs, knocking in 130 runs.

In the Series that fall, they were forced to go to some fairly heroic lengths. They dropped the first two games to the Dodgers, but then five Yankee pitchers delivered five complete games in a row: Ford, Tom Sturdivant, Don Larsen, Bob Turley, and Johnny Kucks. Four of them won, including Larsen, who got twenty-seven outs in a row on October 8. He was, noted Casey Stengel, a man who "liked beer" and who sometimes drove his car up a tree in spring training. "The only thing he fears," observed Jimmy Dykes, "is sleep."

In 1957, they won the pennant by seven games but lost the Series in seven games to the Milwaukee Braves. It was exciteing, almost hysterical, stuff. Lew Burdette pitched three victories for Milwaukee; Ford, Larsen and Turley pitched one each for New York; but Warren Spahn pitched the odd game for the Braves and won it with the help of a smudge of shoe polish that "proved" that Nippy Jones had been struck on the foot by a pitched ball.

It was a time when heavyweights traded haymakers, though. In the third game, Bob Buhl tried to pick Mantle off second base, the throw sailed wide, Red Schoendienst lunged for the ball and fell heavily on top of Mantle, who fought him off and ran to third base—with torn ligaments in his shoulder. Later, bad shoulder or no bad shoulder, Mantle hit a 410-foot home run and the Yankees eventually won by 12 to 3.

The next day, Stengel elected to let Sturdivant pitch to the twenty-three-year-old Henry Aaron with two Braves on base and a stiff wind blowing in. "Babe Ruth couldn't hit one out against that wind," Casey reasoned. Three pitches later, Henry hit one against the wind over the left-field wall. "I thought Babe Ruth couldn't hit one out against that wind," Sturdivant lamented in the dugout. And the Old Man replied with flawless logic: "He ain't Babe Ruth."

So it went. In 1958, with the Giants and Dodgers now settled in California and New York crying for balm, the Yankees sort of wobbled to their fourth pennant in a row. They lost three of the first four games of the Series to the Braves, but then somehow pulled it out, with Turley pitching in all three remaining games and winning two of them for a team that batted only .210. To many people, it was the Yankees' finest hour; but it proved a bittersweet victory—the third Series in a row in which they had been extended to the limit of seven games, and the last they would ever win for old Casey Stengel.

It also marked the end of Phase II: in the middle five years, four more pennants but only two Series titles. And the cracks in the facade were growing a little wider.

In 1959, another pause: They won seventy-nine games and lost seventy-five for a playing percentage of .513, the lowest for a Yankee team in thirty-four summers. The Chicago White Sox filled the vacuum by beating out Cleveland for the pennant, and later George Weiss looked back on the collapse and said:

> It was the only year we lost decisively in twelve years of operation. Criticism went on all year and, as a sensitive man, I think that Casey would have quit if it hadn't been for his great desire to beat John McGraw's record as a manager. Most of the criticism was against his two-platooning, but the fact is that we lost that year because of constant injuries to key players like Bill Skowron, Gil McDougald and Andy Carey. Stengel had his first-string lineup intact for less than a month. That was the sole reason we lost.

Whatever the reason, they lost. Then in 1960, they moved into a new decade and into Phase III: five more pennants but only two more victories in the World Series. And by then, Stengel was gone. Ralph Houk replaced him as manager; then Yogi Berra replaced Houk, and finally Yogi was gone, too.

"In later years," Tony Kubek remembers, "Casey's platooning probably became rougher on the young players. He was more difficult with them. I played five different positions before settling at shortstop, but even then I figured he platooned me less than some of the others." Bobby Richardson, the second baseman for the new generation of Yankees, said: "If I started a game, I'd be pulled out almost immediately for a pinch hitter. If I did go to bat once in a game, I was so tense that I tried too hard.'' Clete Boyer, who became the third baseman in Phase III and beyond, once was removed for a pinch hitter the first time he went to bat in a World Series game.

"He had two tempers," said Phil Rizzuto, who conceded that he did not enjoy playing for Stengel by then. "One for the public and writers, and one for the players under him. The players were frequently dressed down in the dugout and clubhouse. He could charm the shoes off you if he wanted to, but he could also be rough. And after the first couple of seasons, he began to believe he had as much 'magic' as the newspapers said he did."

"I guess this means they fired me," Casey reflected accurately at the changing of the guard. "They told me my services were no longer desired because they wanted to put in a youth program as an advance way of keeping the club going. I'll never make the mistake of being seventy years old again."

WHITEY:
Maybe Casey started getting a little uptight as the seasons went by because we couldn't keep on winning every year and because people started second-guessing him more. You know, saying he was getting too old to run the club. But I don't remember us older guys on the ball club getting too uptight. We were just getting older like Casey was. But we were sure of ourselves and our jobs, and we didn't know why the hell everybody else was getting nervous.

We always screwed around from the beginning, but by then people were saying the club was "out of control" or something. But that was the payoff: As long as you were still winning on the field, nobody made too big a deal out of the stunts off the field. Once you began to lose a little on the field, everything that happened off the field suddenly was a "symptom."

I remember the time we clinched a pennant by winning a doubleheader in Kansas City, and we had a big party at the Muehlebach Hotel there. Everybody was pretty loaded when we got on the train to go to Detroit to play out the season. Ryne Duren was kind of a wild man, anyway, and this time on the train he went up to where Ralph Houk and some guys were playing cards and started making a pain in the ass of himself. He kept annoying Houk and saying Ralph wasn't so Goddamned tough, things like that. Finally, he shoved a cigar into Houk's mouth, and that started it good.

Ralph reached up and slapped Duren, and happened to scratch him over his eye with his World Series ring. So Ryne took a swing at him. He was a strong son of a bitch but he was so drunk that the shot went wild. It took a bunch of us guys to drag them apart, but before we finally got Duren into his bunk on the train, he kicked Larsen in the face and caused a hell of a fuss. Ralph took it okay, though. He just said later, "Duren shouldn't drink. When he does, he's a Jekyll and Hyde."

Which is probably what a lot of people thought the whole team was: Jekyll on the ball field and Hyde after hours. I guess one of the people who thought that way the most was George Weiss, because when we got to Detroit we began to notice some strange characters shadowing us. We knew who they were right away—a couple of detectives Weiss hired to keep an eye on us, mainly me and Mickey. They were pretty easy to spot, though. They'd sit in the lobby of the hotel and watch us over the top of their newspapers, like in the movies.

One day I figured we'd have a little fun with them, so I told the other guys who were sitting around the lobby to watch us for a while. Me and Mickey and Darrell Johnson walked across the lobby of the Statler-Hilton and out the front door, real slow, so the two private eyes would be sure to follow us. Then we jumped in a cab and they jumped in a car and started after us. It was a sketch—we just had our driver go around the block, with them on our tail all the way, and then we pulled up at the front door again and strolled back into the lobby.

Once we even went in a church, in the front door and out the back, and these two guys were right there behind us wondering what the hell we were doing in church. They even followed Kubek and Richardson to the Y.M.C.A., but that was no act because Kubek and Richardson were two of the straightest guys who ever played on the Yankees. I mean they were pure. They roomed together, and they'd go play table tennis or something, and that's what they were doing the time they went to the "Y." I think that's when Weiss finally called the detectives off. It was starting to get too ridiculous, and he was getting worse publicity from the detectives than he was from us.

Mickey and I had to watch ourselves, though, because we'd get blamed even if we did something innocent. I'm not saying we always were innocent, but even when we were, we'd get blamed. I guess that was the price we paid for the times we weren't so innocent.

Once we were supposed to leave Detroit for Chicago by train and our road secretary in those days was Bill McCorry, and this was one time he made a mistake—he forgot to change the itinerary for Daylight Saving Time or something like that. Anyway, Mickey and me and John Drebinger of *The New York Times* went down to the train station by taxi, and the guy said when we got there, "The Yankee train left about forty-five minutes ago." Don't ask me how come the rest of the guys made it on time—maybe they got rounded up in the hotel by McCorry and took the team bus. Mickey and I used to go by ourselves in a cab a lot.

This wasn't our fault, missing the train, but there we were and we sure as hell had missed it. So the three of us turned around, took a cab to the airport and flew to Chicago. All the way there, John Drebinger kept screaming about how Mc-

Corry had screwed us up. That turned out to be good for me and Mickey—you know, Drebbie was one of the old pros of the writers, maybe the No. 1 writer we had, and the madder he got, the more we figured he'd run interference for us. So when we walked in the hotel in Chicago, we just kept our mouths shut and let Drebbie do the hollering. And he did more hollering at McCorry than McCorry did at us.

Another time, we weren't so lucky. Mickey and I missed the train going from Cincinnati to Pittsburgh for an exhibition game. What actually happened was we were bouncing around the night before, doing some drinking when the train was leaving.

I was beginning to get worried, but Mickey said, hell, we'll just take a plane in the morning and be okay. So we kept on drinking and we got about forty-five minutes' sleep that night. Then we got up to catch our plane real early, and we were screwed: It was foggy as hell, and nothing was flying. So we hired this cab to drive us to Pittsburgh, because we knew that Casey wouldn't let us miss the ball game and we knew we were in a jam now if we didn't get there on time.

It cost us something like two hundred and fifty bucks, and we got out of the cab at the Pirates' old park, Forbes Field, just as they were getting ready to take the field. I wasn't supposed to be pitching, but the Old Man's got Mickey in the lineup and here's Mickey so hung-over he can't even stand up straight. No kidding, his eyes were all red and he had this awful headache, and he was really sort of weaving around, he was so tired. Casey was so pissed off that he left him in the lineup to show him a lesson. Mickey got up to bat in the first inning; he was so bleary that he couldn't hardly see the ball *or* the pitcher. But he figured he'd get the hell out of there fast, so he ripped at the first pitch the guy threw—and he got all of it. I'll be a son of a bitch if he didn't hit one of the longest home runs they ever saw in Pittsburgh, way the hell and gone over the roof in right field and a mile high.

MICKEY:

My only problem was running around the bases. I wasn't sure I could make it, so I took it real slow and then got the hell out of there.

That happened to me another time, too. There's some people from Dallas named Harold and Rita Cross, and they live on a farm between Washington and Baltimore. I was on the disabled list then, I'd broken my foot or my toe, I don't remember what it was that time. Anyway, I didn't know it then but the next day I was supposed to come off the disabled list and be ready to play—you know, the next day, I'm back. But we weren't even thinking about it. Whitey had just pitched that day, and he pitched a real good game, so we were all happy and loose. Me and Whitey and Dale Long went out to eat with Harold and Rita Cross and a couple of their friends and had a real good time. You know, Whitey didn't have to work the next day; and I was still on the disabled list with my toe, and Dale Long only pinch-hit once in a while, anyway.

So we went to this real good seafood restaurant in Baltimore—I think it was the Chesapeake—and after we got through eating, we took off for Rita and Harold's house out in the country.

We had all this great wine for dinner, too, and I remember they had some of those goat-bags you drink wine out of. So we filled them up with wine after the dinner and took them with us out to the farm. We sat around talking and drinking, and after a while we decided it was getting late so maybe we better stay the whole night and go back in the morning. So Whitey slept upstairs, and Dale slept on the couch or something. I was getting a little sick or something, so I just went outside to get some fresh air.

When I woke up, I was on the front-porch swing and it was like seven o'clock in the morning and colder than hell. So I went inside and woke everybody up, and said we better get started back to town. Harold Cross got up and took us back to the ball park in Baltimore, where we were supposed to play an afternoon game with the Orioles. Well, first he took us to the hotel, but we had missed the bus, so he just drove us out to the ball park. We didn't have time to brush our teeth or comb our hair or anything, we just went straight to the park.

I didn't give much of a damn because I thought I was still on the disabled list with my toe, so naturally I didn't take batting or infield practice or anything. In fact, Hank Bauer was, I think, coaching the Orioles at that time, and I was talking to him before the game because we'd been together on the Yankees so long before he got traded. And he said to me, "Man, you smell bad. Man, you look bad, too. Why don't you go on out to the outfield so's nobody will see you?" So I go on out to the outfield and stand around, and after a while here comes the Baltimore batboy running out to center field. He's carrying a bottle of Lavoris, and he said, "Mr. Bauer said for you to drink some of this." Well, I worked it around my mouth, you know, and washed my mouth out with it real good and then gave it back to him and told him, "Thanks a lot, anyway."

Well, the game got into the seventh or eighth inning and me and Whitey were sitting down at the end of the bench, and the sun was beating right into the dugout and I was asleep by then. But all of a sudden, Whitey's waking me up and saying, "Mickey, wake up, here comes Ralph." Ralph Houk comes walking down to the end of the dugout and says to me, "Hey, can you hit?" And I say, "Yeah, but I didn't think you could use me." And Ralph says, "Yeah, you went back on the active list today."

So then I said right away, "Sure, I can hit," but you know I hadn't taken any batting practice all day or anything, and I was sleeping in the sun most of the game and didn't get any sleep the night before except on Harold Cross's front porch. But anyway, I started looking for my ball cap and I couldn't find it, and finally we found Whitey was sitting on it all the time.

The bill of the cap was crushed together and it looked like hell on my head, but I finally got ready, got my helmet on and went out of the dugout swinging the heavy bat you use in practice. I'm really in the last place I ever thought I'd be in right now—going up to bat in the Goddamned game. And while I'm swinging the bat going out of the dugout, I look across the field and see Bauer sitting in the Oriole dugout just laughing his ass off.

Then I see him go over and talk to the manager, I think it was Billy Hitchcock then, but whoever it was, when I come up to the plate to hit, he goes running out to the pitcher. It was Mike McCormick, Whitey told me later, but I thought it was Dave McNally. I wouldn't have known, anyway, I was so blind then with no sleep. It was a left-handed pitcher, I know that. And I know what they're telling the pitcher: They're telling him, whatever you do, don't walk this guy, he's been out all night and he's got zero chance of getting a hit. It was a pretty high-scoring game, I think like 7 to 7 or maybe 8 to 8 or something like that.

Anyway, he throws me a fast ball up at my eyes and I just take a wild swing at it and I hit it over the center field fence.

All I remember after that was that I'm really having a hard time running around the bases again. I can hardly feel my feet hitting the ground and I am still so tired I'm only half-awake. But when I come around third base, I look over into the Baltimore dugout and Hank Bauer's just sitting there, shaking his head looking at the floor.

WHITEY:
Somebody wanted to know once how many times we got fined, and all I could think to say was, More times than Babe Ruth.

I remember one fine I got; this one was for myself, it

didn't include Mickey or Billy or anybody else. It was at the beginning of the season in 1960, and I forget what it was for, but it was a pretty good one. And I got fined by Topping himself that time. Then, with two weeks left in the season, we're in the middle of a hell of a pennant race. (We lost the year before, and early in '60 the Old Man got sick and had to go to the hospital with a bad virus, so they made Houk the acting manager for a while. Then we got the lead in September and lost it and finally we were all tied for first place with fifteen games to go. I think we hit 193 home runs that year, and set a league record—Mickey got 40 and Roger Maris was with us then and got 39.) Anyway, with two weeks left in the season, Topping calls me into his office and says he's going to give me the fine back. I happened to be pitching against Steve Barber that night, we had a four-game series with Baltimore and we were just about even with them, and Barber used to kill us. So when Topping told me I'd get the money back, I just said thanks. And he said, "You've got to get this ball club started, right now."

Sure enough, I beat Barber that night, 2 to 0, and we won all four games with Baltimore and ended up winning all fifteen that we had left, and we also won the pennant. I don't know if Topping was getting to be a psychologist or what. Maybe he caught it from Casey.

If you were normal, you could stay awake half the night worrying about a lot of things in baseball—the team getting old, the manager getting fired, yourself getting traded or even hit in the face by a line drive.

After Billy got traded in 1957, we started to worry about getting traded. It got worse in 1960 because I was out half the season with a bad arm. But I pitched two shutouts in the Series against Pittsburgh and probably saved myself. My problem was that George Weiss didn't like me and Mickey. Trading you was Weiss's way of breaking up the naughty threesome. Not Mickey—he wouldn't trade him—but me. I was a candidate, I thought.

Things have changed now. You see owners in the locker room every day now. But in those days, you'd see them on opening day or in the World Series and that was it. You'd see Weiss once a year. The rest of the time you'd sit and worry.

I didn't worry about getting hit by a ball until one day in Kansas City when Bob Cerv lined one back at me. It was getting dark and there were a lot of white shirts behind home plate that kept the ball hidden when it was hit.

Cerv belted this one and the ball shot like a bullet through the middle. It ticked my ear and went into center field. I didn't even realize it *was* the ball until the catcher came out and told me. Then I really started to shake on the mound. Cerv told me later that he thought it was going to hit me in the face.

They had a lot of white shirts in the background in Vero Beach, too, where the Dodgers trained. You couldn't see a ball coming back to the mound. So whenever big Frank Howard came up, I'd throw him big slow curves on the inside. I didn't care if he pulled the ball over the palm trees, as long as he didn't smash it back at me.

As for managers, they always lived dangerously. If you were a player, you knew you might get traded; if you were a manager, you knew you were sure to get fired. Maybe they blamed Casey when we lost the 1960 Series to the Pirates and retired him, but he was already seventy years old then and you had to admit he'd had one hell of a career. But after Ralph Houk ran the ball club for the next three years, he was promoted to general manager and they made Yogi the field manager.

I thought Yogi did a hell of a job. I was his pitching coach—both a pitcher and a coach, actually. But we lost the Series that year, it was 1964. I'd pitched only one game, the first of the seven we played. After that, I was useless. My hand was getting numb. For that matter, I wasn't much help in the first game, either.

So flying home from St. Louis, Yogi came back to me in the airplane and said, "Will you be my coach again next year?" I said, "Sure, Yog." And he said, "Thanks." And he got fired the next day.

When things cooled down a few days later, I called him up and said, "Thanks for assuring me of my job, Yog."

I thought he got screwed. You know, everybody counted us out of the pennant race after we blew the series with the White Sox in late August. But we played like crazy in September and made it. Yogi was a good baseball man. He deserved to stay.

Then they hired Johnny Keane from the Cardinals, but we already were starting to lose guys. The decline really started when Kubek and Richardson retired a year apart, and the defense began to go to hell. Also, the free-agent draft was started—and it was aimed at teams with the best farm systems—the Cardinals, Dodgers and Yankees had a couple of hundred guys each, and they were the targets.

I liked Johnny Keane. He was a great man, a decent man, and I pitched a lot for Keane. He just got there at the wrong time.

Some skeptics, like Manager Charlie Dressen of the Tigers, keep remembering that nickname "Slick" and demand to know why he keeps putting his pitching hand in his back pocket. Johnny Keane and Elston Howard argue for the defense while Slick keeps the hand in the pocket—warming it on his "hot water bottle."

Between laughs, these are the times that try men's souls, all right.

After hours, Butch Cassidy and the Sundance Kid try handling the reins on a couple of Delvin Miller's trotters at Pompano Park in Florida. Whitey, who owns horses, thinks he's "setting up" Mickey. But he looks a little worried at his victim's lead in the stretch. (*United States Trotting Association*.)

For indoor sport after hours, they have been known to hoist a few with Toots Shor, restaurateur, adviser and boon companion to the world of celebrities.

Group portrait of nearly 2,000 home runs: Willie Mays, Henry Aaron and Mantle meet in Atlanta and smile over all those pitches they hit "downtown."

In the twilight of two long careers: reflections.
(*Ernest Sisto*, The New York Times.)

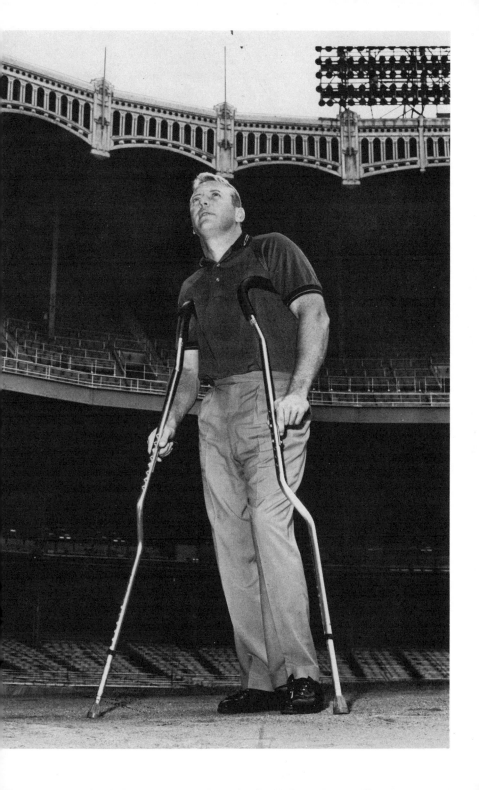

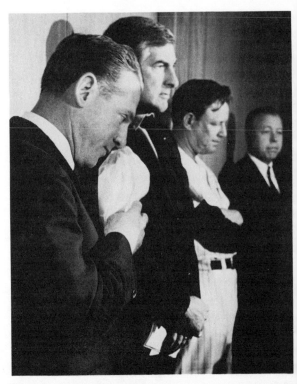

1967: Whitey, who arrived first, departs first—yes, wiping a tear. Mike Burke, Ralph Houk and Lee MacPhail, the Yankee triumvirate, mark the milestone with solemn faces.

1969: Mickey says adieu in the stadium where he started it all, eighteen years earlier. Frank Messer, Joe DiMaggio, Mike Burke and Lee MacPhail watch with mixed emotions as another era of Yankee history ends.

The Country Boy and the City Slicker get the news that they have been elected to the Baseball Hall of Fame— together. It is 1974, a quarter of a century after they arrived— 536 home runs and 236 pitching victories later.

We happy few,
we band of brothers.

WE BAND
OF BROTHERS

$\mathbb{B}$y 1967, the "numbers" were all in: Slick, who threw his first pitch for the team at twenty-one, threw his last at thirty-eight. In between, he worked in 498 ball games—he pitched 3,170 innings—won 236 and lost 106, not counting the World Series.

By the end of 1968, the numbers were all in for Mick, too. He took his first cuts when he was nineteen, his last when he was thirty-seven. In between, he played in 2,401 ball games for the Yankees, went to bat 8,102 times, made 2,415 hits—536 of them home runs. He also walked 1,734 times and struck out just about the same number of times, like 1,710, which adds up to 3,400-and-something walks and strikeouts. "I mustn't have been so hot," he reflected a little guiltily, "because I spent seven years without ever hitting the ball."

When he *was* hitting the ball, he pumped it over a fence left-handed 373 times and right-handed 163 times; at home 266 times, on the road 270 times. In ten games, he hit them out both ways. Seventy times, he hit one out with two men on base; nine times with three.

One of his left-handed home runs was unusual because he

got a little help on it from the pitcher: Denny McLain, the boy wonder who became the boy wastrel. It happened on September 19, 1968, in Tiger Stadium, Detroit. McLain was safely ahead in the eighth inning by 6 to 1, needing only six outs to pitch his thirty-first victory of the season. The Tigers already had clinched the American League pennant—the night before, in fact. So there wasn't much at stake except for Mantle, who needed one home run to pass Jimmy Foxx's career mark of 534.

Everybody figured this was Mantle's last year in a baseball uniform, and so this was his last time at bat in Detroit. And, with a fine sense of history—but not much sense of propriety—McLain watched Mantle give a vague sort of signal for a fast ball over the plate, and obliged by steering a nice fat medium fast ball down the pike. Mantle obliged, too, whacking the ball into the upper seats in right field for No. 535, placing him temporarily in third place on the home-run list behind Babe Ruth (714) and Willie Mays (585).

Nobody cared to admit that Denny had "grooved" one. But as Mickey circled the bases, he tossed a hand-salute to McLain, who later confessed: "That Mantle—he was my idol."

WHITEY:
You know the way Jack Nicklaus can remember every shot he took in a golf tournament? Well, I think I could tell you just about every pitch I threw in those 3,170 innings. And Mickey could tell you just about every pitch that was thrown to him, even if he says sometimes he was too hung-over to know *who* was throwing the ball. Don't let him put you on—most guys have this total recall about the things they saw or did in ball games.

As for the things we saw or did *after* the ball games, me and Mickey have pretty good "recall" there, too. And it's probably a good thing it's not total: There's a lot of those things I'd just as soon not remember. But when you go back over all those seasons, and if somebody asks "Where were you when Larsen was throwing his perfect game?"—you can tell about it from where you were sitting or standing or playing, and maybe nobody else in the world can tell it just that way.

Okay, take Larsen's perfect game. It was in the Series in 1956, right? Everybody remembers that, and maybe most people can tell you it was the fifth game of the Series and he pitched it in Yankee Stadium, and maybe they even know the series was all tied up, two games apiece, between us and the Dodgers. But how many remember that the other pitcher was Sal Maglie, and that we got only five hits off of him? One by Bauer, one by Collins, another by Carey, one by Billy Martin and one by Mickey—and that one was a home run.

Mickey even made a good play catching a ball in left-center that might've broken up the no-hitter. What I remember, though, is that Casey had me down in the bullpen that afternoon; it was sort of unusual for me to relieve in a game, but this was the World Series and Larsen had some problems in the late innings that year. So they had me down there warming up in the sixth, seventh, eighth, and even the ninth inning. If he got the first guy out, sometimes I'd stop throwing and sit down. Well, hell, he got all the first guys out, of course—he got everybody out—so I'd stop throwing and then sit down and watch.

It was pretty quiet in the pen, too. You couldn't see much of the field from the bullpen because it was out there behind right field, but after the fourth or fifth inning we knew it was a perfect game he was working on. Close, too. We only got one run off Maglie in the fourth and another in the sixth, and won it, 2 to 0.

After the game, Larsen had plaques made up, showing a photo of himself pitching in the ninth with two down and two strikes and two balls on the last hitter, Dale Mitchell. Each of the ball players on the team got one as a souvenir from Larsen, and remember, this was a guy people thought was a wild man sometimes. So I guess even a wild man has memories he wants to keep.

I remember 1961, too, because that was maybe the wildest year any of us went through. It was the best year I ever had, for one thing—I went 25 and 4—and we got in a close pennant race with Detroit. They had Bob Scheffing as their manager and we played them three games in September and won all three. But the whole year was kind of relaxing for us because it was Ralph Houk's first season as our manager after Casey retired, or got fired or whatever it was, and Ralph was one of the players and the guys really loved him.

I remember the winter before that season, I ran into Ralph and Bette at a basketball game at Madison Square Garden and went over to congratulate him on getting the job. He'd been coaching first base for a while before that. And he told me, "I want you to pitch every fourth day next season." I'd never done that, usually I worked every fifth day. But I said great, because I used to get bored sitting on the bench, anyway, when I wasn't playing. And I wound up having my best year.

A lot of the guys did, too, like Roger Maris—but it wasn't so relaxing for him the way things turned out. In fact, it was a nightmare for him after he got into this thing of catchint up to Babe Ruth's record of sixty home runs.

We only got Maris the year before from Kansas City, where he hit like sixteen home runs, but everybody knew he had terrific power and was a real pro as a ballplayer. In his first game with us, up in Boston, he got four hits and busted his ass hustling a couple of singles into doubles. And I thought, boy, we've really got a good one.

He hit thirty-nine home runs the first year we had him, in 1960, when we got beat in the Series in Pittsburgh when Bill Mazeroski hit one out in the last half of the ninth inning in the seventh game. Then the next year, Casey was gone and Ralph was in charge and we got into this crazy thing with the pennant race and the home runs.

Maris was from out in Fargo, North Dakota, and he was a very friendly guy, even though later he got a bad rap from some of the writers and even some of the fans who resented him. I don't know, it might've been because he wasn't one of the old Yankees and here he was getting more home runs than Babe Ruth *or* Mickey Mantle. But he and Mickey were close, they even lived together for a while in '61, him and Mickey and Bob Cerv. No jealousy or anything, they got along real good.

We still had some fun, even with all the fussing around late in the season. Once, Bob Turley invited a few of us over to his place in Lutherville, Maryland, me and Skowron and Cerv and Maris and Mickey. He had this swimming pool there, and during the afternoon we got talking about things like racing and swimming. Mickey couldn't swim ten feet, but he always tried to kid guys by saying he'd been the Oklahoma state champion in everything. So after a while, Maris said, "Okay, I'll race you in the pool."

Mickey backed off, but I got him off to the side and worked out one of our famous deals. I told him, "Look, I'll be standing on the side of the pool with a pole and I'll pull you down to the end." So he and Maris jumped in and, while Maris was still underwater or swimming straight ahead, I stood on the side with this pole and Mickey caught hold of it and I yanked him the length of the pool, running along the edge. He'd be there at the end before Maris even got to it. He'd lift his head out of the water and be amazed to find Mantle already there.

After a couple of races, Maris started to suspect somebody was cheating. We had to quit it, though, after Mickey started scraping his shoulder along the side of the pool.

Roger and Mickey were all even in home runs in August that year with forty-four and then forty-five. Four days later, Roger hit No. Forty Seven and then forty-eight, and then the pressure started building up. I felt sorry for Roger after that, the last month of the season, and so did Mickey. It really helped Mickey in a way, because they used to boo him pretty good sometimes, and now Maris was getting it. They had somebody new to boo. The writers, TV, radio, fans, everybody began hounding him, and he even began to lose some of his hair. The doctors said it was nerves.

It was unbelievable, every place we went near the end of the year, they had packed stadiums and everybody going crazy. The reporters would flock around Maris and Mantle in the locker room and ask Roger questions like, Are you hitting so many home runs because the ball is livelier now? And Maris would answer something like, "That's a lot of shit." Or some guy would ask for the one-thousandth time, Do you think you'll break Babe Ruth's record? And he'd stare back and answer, for the one-thousandth time, "I don't care about the fucking record. All I want to do is win the pennant." He meant it, too, but whatever he said was taken the wrong way.

None of the players, though, felt Maris was an outsider who had no "right" breaking Ruth's record. They were all pulling for both him and Mickey to do it. Then one day in September, it got to be just Roger by himself because Mickey was hurting in his knees the way he always did and he got this real heavy cold and virus. Some doctor in New York gave him a penicillin shot or something in the behind, and a couple of days later he got an infection where the needle went in. Sidney Gaynor was our team doctor, and he took a look and said you could've put a golf ball in where the infection was. They had to cut it out, and Mickey missed a couple of weeks of the pennant race and finished up with fifty-four home runs.

Roger kept hitting them, though, and I was in the bullpen when he got his sixty-first and broke the record. I think the whole pitching staff was there; we went out to the bullpen because some guy had offered a lot of money to whoever caught the ball. When he hit it, we all jumped up and jockeyed around trying to catch it, but it landed in the grandstand maybe fifteen or twenty feet to the right, and some kid caught it.

Later, Roger said that in Kansas City once he went 6-for-110 without getting booed, but now with the Yankees he was going good and getting booed all the time. They even used to heave stuff at him. One guy in Detroit broke off the arm of a seat in the ball park and threw it at him on the field, no kidding.

MICKEY:
Once, when Roger was taking all that heat, he even got a big list of questions that was sent to New York from some paper in Japan by cable, and he said, "No wonder I'm going nuts." Another time, some writer asked him, "What's a .260 hitter like you doing hitting all those home runs?" And Maris just looked at him and said, "You've got to be a fucking idiot." After a while, he came to me and said, "I can't take it any more, Mick." And I had to tell him, "You'll have to take it, you'll just have to."

Look, I knew he'd have to take it because they'll boo the ass off of anybody sometimes. I used to get it, too, and in Yankee Stadium besides. They'd get on me for not going in the army or not being able to run so fast if my legs were bad.

One guy even booed me and Willie Mays at the same time. It was in '62 in the Series. The year before, when Maris and me were hitting the home runs, we beat Cincinnati in the Series. Then we played the Giants in '62, the year it kept raining out in San Francisco and they had to keep putting off the game for three days. Maybe that's what happened to me: the more it rained, the more me and Whitey and the guys horsed around in San Francisco. Anyway, all the papers were writing about how the Series had these two great center fielders, Mays and Mantle, and the way it turned out, neither one of us was doing too Goddamn good.

So one day I'm out in center field and I hear this big booming voice yelling at me, "Hey, Mantle. Everybody came out here to see which was better, you or Mays. Now we wonder which one of you guys is worse.''

The next inning, I grounded out and now I'm hitting like .100 for the series, and I go back out to center and now this same guy yells over, "Hey, Mantle, you win. *You're* the worst.''

Sometimes you even get it from the family, and that's when it really hurts. Once I struck out three times in a game and, when I got back to the clubhouse, I just sat down on my stool and held my head in my hands, like I was going to start crying. I heard somebody come up to me, and it was little Timmy Berra, Yogi's boy, standing there next to me. He tapped me on the knee, nice and soft, and I figured he was going to say something nice to me, you know, like ''You keep hanging in there,'' or something like that.

But all he did was look at me and then he said in his little kid's voice, ''You stink.''

WHITEY:

I guess we didn't realize it then, but we weren't going to win the Series any more after 1962 with Willie and the Giants. The Dodgers beat us four straight in '63 and the Cardinals beat us in seven in '64. And after that, we didn't even get in it.

We still did some dumb things, though, like the time we were up in Minnesota when Billy Martin was working in the front office there before he started managing. He did some guy a favor, going to a Little League dinner or something, and the guy wanted to pay him back. Billy wouldn't take any money, so the guy said, "Look, you got some friends. Any time you want to have a good time, take them out to Armstrong's Game Farm and just send me the bill for whatever you shoot.'' The guy was a member of this club where you paid to shoot and fish—so much for a duck, so much for a quail or a goose.

So Billy took us out and we started fishing in the morning, pretty early in the morning, with three of us in a rowboat.

They had to screw around, as usual. They told me to row first, on this lake that was maybe five hundred yards long and maybe a hundred yards wide. They put these lines in the water and started fishing, and I kept rowing, and then I kept saying, "Who's going to row next?" But they were having so much fun catching bass that they kept me rowing. I was getting blisters on my hands by now, but they kept me rowing till they caught enough fish and then said, "Okay, let's go in," and I hadn't even fished yet.

Next we went hunting, and Billy and me and Mickey got joined by some of the Twins players, Harmon Killebrew and Bob Allison, and their farm director, Sherry Robertson. It was unreal because they had all these birds there, like Canada geese that cost you about fifteen bucks if you shot one. But after a while, the geese and the ducks were just laying all over the place, we must've shot fifty ducks and all seven Canada geese they kept stocked there. And then we go out in the field and shoot quail and chukkers, a bunch of them.

Now I've been shooting the shotgun all afternoon, and it's been hitting me right in the shoulder whenever I'd fire, plus I've got these blisters all over my hands. Then we head for the ball park about five-thirty and I'm supposed to pitch that night, but when I'm putting on my sweatshirt I can see that my hands are all blisters and my shoulder is all black and blue where the gun butt kept hitting it.

I didn't even think I could lift my arm, but anyway I pitched and beat them, 2 to 0. So later I went over to Ralph and told him what happened, and he said, "You son of a bitch. It's a good thing you won." And it was, because the next day I really couldn't lift my arm, it was so stiff and sore. The only guy who hurt more was probably the guy who told Billy to send him the bill at the club.

After that, we didn't bounce around so much because we were probably getting older, and after a while, me and Mickey were the only guys left on the team from the first few seasons. I really hurt my arm in the Series in 1964 and that

October, right after the Series, I went down to Houston for an operation. Denton Cooley, the famous surgeon, repaired the circulation under my left arm.

When they opened the Astrodome in 1965, and we went from spring training in Florida to Puerto Rico for a couple of exhibition games, then back to Florida, then across to Houston and finally up to Minnesota, where we opened the season on the road. But they had the Yankees and the Baltimore Orioles play the Astros that weekend when they opened the new ball park with the roof.

Johnny Keane was our manager then; he was a serious and straight man we got from the Cardinals after they beat us in the Series. They had President Johnson in the Astrodome for the first game, and Keane made Mickey the lead-off batter so he could get the first swings in the first ball park with a roof on it. Mickey did okay, too, he got the first swing and the first hit, and later, he even got the first home run there.

But like I said, by that time we were already in what they call the "decline" of the Yankees, only we didn't know it. I guess maybe we had an idea everything was changing, because you could see we weren't replacing guys the right way. Kubek and Richardson retired when they were only around thirty, and we got nothing back. Maris got traded a couple of years later, and we got Charlie Smith for him. Joe Pepitone and Clete Boyer got traded, and nobody took their place, and finally me and Mickey had to retire—and you don't get anything back when a guy just quits.

Take our lineup from the 1961 World Series. We had Skowron at first base, Bobby at second, Boyer at third, Kubek at short, Hector Lopez in left, Mantle in center and Maris in right, with Yogi catching. Or, Yogi in left field maybe when Elston was catching. Well, the only guy on that club who was *not* brought up in the Yankee system was Maris, which shows the strength of the system.

But the difference is that by 1974, say, we were playing Baltimore and I noticed they had ten guys in the lineup, including the designated hitter, and the only guy *not* brought up in their chain was Tommy Davis. But by then, I looked at our own lineup and saw only two guys, Thurman Munson and Bobby Murcer, who were Yankee system players. And this was like ten years after we won our last pennant. The farm system just didn't supply enough replacements when the team started getting old.

Yeah, me and Mickey got old, too. In the 1964 Series, I was pitching the first game in St. Louis and I had a 4-to-2 lead when they got four runs off me in the bottom of the sixth. Suddenly my left hand went numb; it just went dead. No blood was getting down from the shoulder: the artery was blocked. The blood was just coming down through the little capillaries, and I didn't have a pulse for a year.

I went to Dr. Cooley and he thought it was just wear and tear that caused it, a little injury in the artery that maybe Mother Nature kept healing from the inside, till the artery got completely blocked. They deflated one of my lungs in the operation, went in under my left shoulder and pinched a nerve in my back with a silver clip. Dr. Cooley thought that by leaving the capillaries open enough blood would get through. They usually alternate open and closed. Well, there wasn't a big enough supply of blood that way, so the next year I went back and he did a bypass operation. Took a vein out of my left leg and hooked it into my left shoulder. He woke me up in intensive care after the operation and said, "Feel it. You've got a pulse again."

Before he fixed it for good that time, my fingers would get numb when I pitched. So I had this little bottle of hot water that I'd use to warm my fingers on. Once when we were playing against Detroit, Charlie Dressen, their manager, came out to the mound on opening day in Yankee Stadium and said I couldn't use it. I said, "Hey, Charlie, why not? I don't do anything with it but warm my fingers." But he said no, it wasn't legal under the rules. Maybe he thought I was throwing a wet one with it, I don't know. It was only a little nose-spray bottle that our trainer, Joe Soares, would fill with hot water every inning.

Anyway, Dressen wouldn't let me use it to keep my fingers warm, and I finally said something like "you son of a bitch, why not?" It was sad. Not long after that, Charlie had a heart attack and died. I always hated the idea that those were the last words I ever said to him.

Compared to Mickey, though, I was lucky because he always played with a lot of pain. He had bad knees all the time he was with the Yankees. Once I was sitting at the bar in the Hotel Cleveland with Bill Kane, who's the traveling secretary of the club now, and he has this real bad leg—you know, it's a lot thinner than the other one and Bill walks with a limp. Anyway, we were having a few drinks there at the bar and the way Bill had his legs crossed, his pants were up a little and you could see this tiny, thin ankle on his bad leg.

Then this drunk guy comes up to us at the bar and right away he recognizes me, but he thinks Bill Kane is Mickey Mantle. Maybe that's the way people in Cleveland always figured it: If the Yankees were in town and two guys were drinking at the bar, it had to be Ford and Mantle. Anyway, Kane and I played along with him and didn't let on that Bill really wasn't Mantle, and this guy keeps talking away and all for about ten minutes and was starting to get annoying.

All of a sudden, he looks down and he sees this thin leg of Bill's and then looks straight up in his face and says, like he got struck with religion, "Mickey, I know you went through a lot of pain but, by God, I don't think the fans around the country realize how bad your legs really are." And after that, I always pictured this guy going back to his hometown and telling everybody that he met Mickey Mantle and what great courage Mick must've had to run on a leg like that one.

I'll tell you, though, he wasn't too far wrong. If I have any lasting picture of Mickey myself, it's probably a picture of a really strong, powerful guy with all these muscles—and with two of the worst knees you ever saw. Sometimes we'd be sitting and talking or having dinner, and he'd be there sort of rubbing his knees with his hand, and then when it came time to get up and leave, he'd take a long, long while just lifting up out of his chair, like it was killing him to put all that weight on those bad knees. I think he was in pain all the time I knew him.

MICKEY:

Back in Oklahoma when I was a kid in high school, I was maybe fifteen years old, I got hurt the first time in a football game. Somebody kicked me in the left ankle, and later they found I had this bone disease, osteomyelitis. I went in the hospital a couple of times and they treated it and then said it was okay—I mean, it was arrested, but could always come back, like it was hanging there waiting. And that's why the army wouldn't take me, even after I got with the Yankees and they asked the draft board to give me another check-up to see if I could go in. They said no way, but I still used to get letters from people asking what the hell I was doing playing ball for all that money instead of going in the army.

Then in the World Series in 1951, my first season with the Yankees, I tripped on that water-main sprinkler in the out-field—when I was holding back so DiMaggio could catch the ball that Willie Mays hit—and I twisted my knee and got torn ligaments. That was the start of my knee operations. I had four. You start out with two sets of cartilage in each knee; now I've only got one set left. Once they operated on my shoulder and tied the tendons together. I had a cyst cut out of my right knee another time. And down in Baltimore in 1962, Slick was pitching one night and Brooks Robinson hit a home run over the center-field fence. I jumped up and tried to catch it before it went over, and got my foot caught in the wire mesh on the fence, and that time I broke my foot about halfway up.

I guess the army figured they'd have to pay me a pension for life if they ever took me with those bad wheels. But I wish I'd gone in and got the two years over with, and not have taken all the heat about being a 4-F.

The worst thing, though, was that very first time when I got hurt in the '51 Series because my father came in from Oklahoma to see me play, and when they got me to the hospital I found out my Dad was sick a lot worse than me.

My knee was swelled up so bad after it got twisted that they sent me to the hospital in a cab with my Dad. We called him Mutt—his real name was Elven, but everybody called him Mutt when he was playing ball out home. He was damned good, too, but he had to work in the mines all his life, so I guess he started hoping that I'd be able to do what he hadn't done. He even named me Mickey after Mickey Cochrane because I was born in 1931 when Cochrane was one of the big stars on the Philadelphia A's.

Anyway, Dad and I pulled up to Lenox Hill Hospital in this cab and he got out first to help me out. So I put my arm around his shoulders to get out the door and put my weight on him, and he just collapsed on the sidewalk. They took him in and found out he had Hodgkin's disease, and it already had eaten up his whole back.

I got operated on and then we went home, and he went back to work. But I could tell he was really sick then. So after I got better, I took him up to the Mayo Clinic, and they cut him open and then sewed him back up again and said just to let him do whatever he wanted because he didn't have much longer to live. He went back home to the mines and worked about a month, and died in May the following year. He was the bravest man I ever knew, he never complained, he never acted scared.

He was thirty-nine when he died, and my two uncles died before they reached forty, too. So I figured, you know, maybe it sort of runs in the family. But I loved my father so much that I always wanted to please him, and I guess that's why all he had to do was get sore at me when I got sent down to the minors by Casey that time. I couldn't stand it for him to be so disappointed with me. So I decided to stay and try to make it work out.

It's like I said: All he had to do was look at me, and I knew what was right and wrong.

Later, Casey became like a father to me, maybe because I was only nineteen years old when I started playing for him and a couple of years later my own Dad was gone. The Old Man helped me a lot, I guess he even protected me, and by the time he left the Yankees, I had a few very good years behind me. But I still didn't have it in my head that I was a good major-league ballplayer.

Then Ralph Houk came along and changed my whole idea of thinking about myself. I mean, off the field I used to screw around a lot with Slick, but on the ball field I still didn't have no real confidence. Not till Houk came along and told me, "You are going to be my leader. You're the best we've got."

CASEY STENGEL:

He was fairly amazing in several respects, and he commenced showing it when he was still a kid. He had all that power from both sides, which not many men have, since they're either right-handed or left-handed, and even then they can't always hit it over a building. What it means is the pitcher can't pitch around anybody with Mantle coming up. He could hurt you either way, and who else can do that?

You couldn't catch him going down to first base, either—even with those bad legs of his. And he could throw good and he'd catch the ball in the outfield and later, after Di-Maggio left, he got to be the big man on the ball club. If he didn't have those knees, he might've played long after most other men were gone.

You take Ford, the first day he come up, he thought he owned the place. He knew how to pitch, and he didn't waste a lot of time doing it. Let me ask you, if it takes twenty-seven outs to win, who's going to get them out more ways than Mr. Ford? And he didn't hurt himself doing it too often.

They weren't too much alike when they joined the club because Ford looked so sure of himself and Mantle thought he should've been watching from the seats instead of center field. But it was amazing how they got to be alike later, which is remarkable for me to say with so many great ball players, and even with weak knees and weak circulation they both could do it. They could beat you.

JERRY COLEMAN:
The big thing was, Mickey had this theory about not living long. When we were roommates, I was into player relations and pensions, but he'd say, "I'll never get one. I won't live long enough."

WHITEY:
The other day, Marvin Miller was over at the clubhouse talking about the players' pension plan, how you could start collecting when you got to be fifty. And Mickey kept saying, "Get it cut down to forty." And before that, when he was in his thirties, he'd say, "Boy, they better get that thing cut down to forty."

He always had it in his mind that he wasn't going to make it to forty because of his uncles and his father. But I told him, "You're forty-three years old now and you never thought you'd make it to forty, so you got three years of gravy."

He really used to worry about it. We'd sit in the room and he used to talk more about that probably than anything else. I'd say, "Goddamn it, your father and your uncles never went to the Mayo Clinic every year for a check-up, and they worked in the mines and were probably getting that stuff in their lungs all the time. So it doesn't mean that just because they died at thirty-eight or thirty-nine, you will, too. You'll probably outlive us all."

I really think that's why Mickey acted a little crazy at

times. It wasn't what Toots Shor said when we got voted into the Hall of Fame: "It shows what you can accomplish if you stay up all night drinking whiskey all the time."

It wasn't that. I think Mickey acted a little crazy at times because he just figured he was only going to be around a little while and he might as well enjoy it.

MICKEY:
Then why did you act a little wild at times, too?

WHITEY:
Just to keep you company, Mick, just to keep you company.

MICK, SLICK, AND COOL PAPA

They were an unlikely bunch, standing there in the sunshine that morning in the Last-of-the-Mohicans country of upstate New York—Mick, Slick and Cool Papa Bell. And, of all people, an umpire, Jocko Conlan, who proved again that he could not bite the hand that fed him by voicing thanks to "Almighty God and the committee that voted me in."

It was August 12, 1974, and "the committee" had voted Jocko into the Hall of Fame, the baseball shrine in Cooperstown at the tip of Lake Otsego where old Abner Doubleday certainly did *not* invent baseball. But if baseball did not start there, it ended there for the best of the bunch who played the game for a living.

Not many made it, and sometimes even those who made it weren't around to stand in the sunshine and take the final bow. Like Sam Thompson, who hit 128 home runs in the National League before the turn of the century, and Sunny Jim Bottomley, who hit 219 home runs after the turn of the century. In fact, as the crowd applauded the four who were there and the two who weren't, the number of niches and plaques inside the brick building reached just 146.

But whether Doubleday started the ball rolling or not, this was a day for creating legends, not shooting them down. The Commissioner of Baseball, a six-foot-five-inch Princeton lawyer named Bowie Kuhn, pronounced it "the greatest day in the baseball year." And he got no guff—not from the six new figures being inducted, not from the twenty-one old-time players on the platform who had preceded them, not from Jim Bottomley's widow, Sam Thompson's nephew, Babe Ruth's wife, Christy Mathewson's niece, Lou Gehrig's wife, the House of Representatives' John Conlan Jr. or Henry Aaron's secretary of state, Donald Davidson. And especially not from old Casey Stengel in his bright red blazer.

He got no guff because, greatest day or not, it was a day that turned people's minds from the momentous events that Washington had been producing, especially in the last few days: Richard Nixon resigning as President, Gerald Ford taking over as President. But there in the boondocks, people were standing on the grass lawn trying to relive some of the easier moments. All eyes rested on the little stage taken over by Mantle of Oklahoma, Ford (no relative) of Manhattan, Conlan of Chicago, and Bell of Starkville, Mississippi. They were "going in," with Sunday manners and Sunday clothes; and whenever one of the speakers started to list the *reasons* they were going in, Stengel would turn in his camp chair, wink at nobody in particular, and add some punctuation by saying, in a gravel stage whisper, "and that's the damned truth."

It was the damned truth, all right, that they all had got there the hard way. Take James Bell. Like the others, poor when he began playing ball; unlike the others, black, which explained why he had played ball for a living for twenty-nine summers and twenty-one winters. He wouldn't have made it at all, except for the fact that three years earlier they had decided to elect heroes of the old Negro Leagues. So now he was passing through the gates surrounded by Satchel Paige, Roy Campanella, Buck Leonard, and Monte Irvin, who also had made it long after the fact.

"I was a kid when I started with the St. Louis Stars in 1922," Bell remembered, "and they figured I'd be afraid of the big crowd. But I wasn't, so they began to call me 'Cool.' But the manager said that wasn't enough of a name, so he wanted to add something to it, and I became Cool Papa.

"There were a lot of great ones in the Negro Leagues," he told the audience, not injecting any bitterness into the sunny occasion but injecting some sadness into it. "We—Satchel, Irvin, Campy, Leonard and myself—were the lucky ones. I'm thanking God for letting me smell the roses while I'm still living."

They had said the same thing about Casey Stengel eight years earlier when they waived the customary five-year waiting period required for baseball canonization and voted him into the Hall of Fame: They let him smell the roses while he was still living. He got the votes by a sort of national acclamation, not for any records he had fractured as a ball player, not for the syntax he had fractured as a public orator, but for fifty years of doing *everything* on a grander scale than anybody else. And most particularly for steering the Yankees through their ten pennants and seven world championships during his twelve years as the helmsman.

By then, nobody blamed him for steering the Mets through four or five last-place finishes in a row—a streak that was not diminished even after the Professor fell, broke his hip and was finally succeeded by Wes Westrum, one of his coaches who used to catch for the New York Giants. Indeed, when Stengel appeared in the Mets' training camp the spring after his retirement, he was still talking a blue streak with no hint that his style had been overpowered by his own impending election to Cooperstown.

"This club's got a chance to move," he remarked approvingly, with no trace of resentment over his new role on the sidelines of baseball. "These fellows aren't as green as when I had them. You won fifty games last year, didn't you? Then why didn't you win sixty? That's what I'd like to know.''

"The last coaches were terrific men,'' he went on, whether you were ready or not. "Two of them got employed running other clubs—three, counting our man. And now, can you fulfill the job?''

But his references, and his thoughts, always seemed to slip back before the start of the Mets—to the finish of the Yankees. *His* finish, anyway. Without pausing to identify Bill Virdon, the Mets' new farm-team manager at Williamsport, or Dick Groat, who had been Virdon's teammate on the Pittsburgh Pirates, he plunged ahead:

"Now you got Virdon, a splendid high-class fella, and there's got to be something wrong with the outfield which he can help these young men. And his roommate at Pittsburgh was Groat, and they beat us out of the World Series and I got discharged.''

That's what it always came back to, the Yankee years, whether he was limping off the scene leaning on a cane or standing alongside Ted Williams outside the Hall of Fame on the morning *they* were enshrined for vastly different reasons.

The Commissioner of Baseball then was William D. Eckert, a onetime air force general, a proper, erect, almost guarded man in a dark suit and wintry smile. He introduced Stengel as the one hundred and fourth person to be installed at Cooperstown, then ducked while Casey made his valedictory.

"Mr. Eckert,'' he began in acknowledgement when the cheering had subsided, "and those distinguished notables that are sitting on the rostrum. I want to thank everybody. I want to thank some of the owners who were amazing to me, and those big presidents of the leagues who were kind to me when I was so obnoxious. I want to thank everybody for my first managerial experience at Worcester, which was last in the Eastern League, and where I met that fine fellow George Weiss, who ran the New Haven club and who would find out whenever I was discharged and would re-employ me.

"I want to thank my parents for letting me play baseball, and I'm thankful I had baseball knuckles and couldn't become a dentist.

"I got $2,100 a year when I started in the big league and lived at Broadway and Forty-seventh Street. And they get more money now.

"I chased the balls that Babe Ruth hit. We couldn't play on Sundays, that was the preacher's day to collect. But in Baltimore we played at a racetrack even, and Ruth hit one over my head and Robby said, 'You'd think you'd play back on a guy who swings like that.' So I replied, 'Who's Babe Ruth? He's a kid who just came out of that school.' But I backed up fifty feet more and called over to Hy Myers, 'Far enough?' And he said okay. And Ruth hit it way over my head just the same.''

It always seemed to get back to Babe Ruth, too, whenever they got around to comparing things past and present. And even on the sunny morning eight years later, when Stengel in his blazing red jacket sat on the same platform listening to other speeches, they were still talking back to the era when Ruth built the Yankees and the Yankees owned the ball.

Mantle, mellowing at forty-two, made sure that his family and friends would be there listening: He hired a bus that took the caravan 250 miles from the Essex House on Central Park South in New York to the site of the Hall of Fame, up where James Fenimore Cooper's settlers used to dodge his Mohicans. There was Merlyn and their four boys—Mickey, David, Billy, and Danny—and Mickey's mother, all arrayed in the front row. And Ford, mellowing slightly at forty-five, made sure that *he'd* make it by taking the Red-eye Special out of Los Angeles late Saturday night after the Yankees had played the California Angels. He was a coach then, stopping just long enough in New York to pick up Joan and Tommy and Sally Ann, plus his mother Edith and a batch of uncles and in-laws, then driving up the Thruway to join the crowd.

After Cool Papa Bell had reminisced about his twenty-nine

summers and twenty-one winters on the ball fields of the black leagues, they introduced the pitcher who had broken Babe Ruth's record of shutout innings in World Series games, and Whitey stepped to the microphone while Mantle and Stengel sat back to listen.

"I walked down the aisle three weeks ago with my daughter," he said, "and thought I was nervous then. But between what happened in Washington last week and what happened here in Cooperstown today, I'd have to say it was a pretty good week for the Fords.

"I've been a Yankee fan since I was five years old, and there are a lot of people I want to thank. My family, sitting here in front. My wife Joan, my mother, my daughter Sally Ann and her husband Stephen, and Eddie at Elmira in the Red Sox organization, and Tommy, who's a cameraman at Shea Stadium. The Yankee organization, playing for such men as George Weiss, Dan Topping, now George Steinbrenner. And, of course, Casey."

He paused, not letting sentiment get the best of the situation, and added: "And I want to thank my teammates—like Mantle, Roger Maris and Yogi Berra—for scoring all those runs, even though Mickey says that if I hadn't thrown so many long fly balls in center field, he could have played ten years more."

Then Mantle went to the center of the stage and, after the cheering had finally died down, he said:

"We didn't have a lot of money when I was a kid. We moved out of the town of Commerce to a farm, and my twin brothers and I used to chase baseballs in a pasture. My mother used to make my uniforms—that's how poor we were. When I started playing for the Baxter Springs Whiz Kids—with that name on the shirt—I really thought that was something. It was the first uniform she didn't make for me."

He told how Tom Greenwade had been passing through Oklahoma "to see a guy play in Broken Bow," and how the Yankee scout had stopped off long enough to watch Mantle pump three home runs out of sight. And how he had come back a year later, "the night I graduated."

He remembered that he had not always been too lucky in business, even after joining the Yankees and playing in a dozen World Series. A lot of the business deals didn't pan out, even though he once contributed an original slogan for a fried-chicken chain of country kitchens that carried his name. Merlyn Mantle, sitting up front, winced as he laughed at her embarrassment and quoted his own gem, "To get a better piece of chicken, you'd have to be a rooster."

Then, skipping past the 536 home runs and all the other statistics, he invoked the name that counted at the Yankee reunions: "I broke Babe Ruth's record for strikeouts. He struck out only 1,500 times. I did it 1,710 times. That's one record nobody will break. If you strike out that often, they don't let you play."

Stengel turned aside in his folding chair and gave his version of "amen," saying to nobody in particular again, "And that's the damned truth."

It took Mantle and Ford a long time to get off the platform because people pinned them down and there was no way to escape for a while. Mantle reached into his pocket at one point and drew out a set of pages that contained his "other" speech—a Rabelesian thing that duly "thanked" a long list of people who had helped him in his career. One of the milder paragraphs thanked Hank Bauer "for teaching me how to drink." It was an underground speech that deteriorated sharply from there. He said he'd been tempted for a time to deliver it from the stage, but his sense of history— and Ford's sense of outrage—kept it in his pocket while he was playing it straight. If he *had* switched to the earthy version, Stengel would have had a lot more chances to make it a litany by chanting his line, "and that's the damned truth."

But Mick's "underground" speech never surfaced, and the lasting glimpse he gave the throng that morning was polished, poised, confident, and properly aware of what was happening. He tried to leave the platform, but his path was blocked by the entourage besieging Stengel, and then Ford was at his side saying:

"Sally Ann and Steve had the room next door to the Old Man last night, and in the middle of the night they could hear Casey shouting things like 'He was safe, and the shortstop was out of position for the tag, anyway!' They figure he was still shooting down the umpires in his sleep."

He turned to Mantle, raising an eyebrow, and said: "I was in bed tossing and turning all night, worrying about my speech. Where did you go after dinner?"

"I was downstairs all night with young Mickey and your Tommy," Mantle said, sounding like a gentleman of leisure, carefree among the weak-kneed of the world. "Playing pool, drinking beer till the sun came up."

"You had the right idea—drink beer and shoot pool all night," Ford said, conceding the point. "If I'd known what you guys were doing downstairs, I'd have been there with you instead of worrying about my speech. I blew it."

Mantle laughed out loud, like a horse snorting, and tried again to push his way through the crowd. Ford tried to follow, got stacked up in the pile of people, then shrugged and said:

"It's been always like this, ever since I first saw him taking those swings in the cage in St. Louis and Chicago back in '50. Once he got the hang of it, he was the same way, whether it was the night before opening day or the World Series. Or Cooperstown.

"Come to think of it, we never said anything to each other about getting into Cooperstown. We were never like that. When one of our wives had a baby, we wouldn't congratulate each other. We'd just go out and get drunk."

Finally they shoved their way through the crowd on the stage and reached for the double doors leading inside the Hall of Fame building. Stengel was there, breaking free of the swarm, so they paused and held the door open for their eighty-four-year-old manager. They bowed slightly from the waist, as though on cue, and Casey stopped and gave them a satisfied look of appraisal. Then all three passed through the doors while the Professor said to nobody in particular:

"Yes sir, they were fairly amazing in several respects, and that's the damned truth."

APPENDIX

EDWARD CHARLES (Whitey) FORD

Born October 21, 1928, at New York, N.Y.
Height, 5.10. Weight, 181.
Blue eyes and blond hair.
Threw and batted lefthanded.
Married Joan Foran, April 14, 1951.
Hobby—Golf.

Tied major league record for most consecutive one-hit games (2), September 2 and 7, 1955.
Holds American League record for lowest earned-run average, league, 200 or more games won (2.74), 1967.
Tied American League record for most consecutive games won, rookie season (9), July 17 to September 25, 1950, second game.
Led American League in complete games with 18 in 1955 and led in shutouts with 7 in 1958.
Holds the following World Series records: Most Series played by pitcher (11); most games pitched, total Series (22); most putouts, total Series (11); most putouts by pitcher, four-game Series (3); most games started (22); most opening games started (8); most games lost, total Series (8); most innings pitched, total Series (146); most bases on balls, total Series (34); most strikeouts, total Series (94); all marks as of 1964 Series.
Named as Pitcher on *The Sporting News* All-Star Major League teams, 1955–56.
Named as Pitcher on *The Sporting News* American League All-Star teams, 1961–63.
Named American League Pitcher of the Year by *The Sporting News*, 1955–61–63.
Won Cy Young Memorial Award, 1961.

YEAR	Club	League	G	IP	W	L	PCT.	H	R	ER	SO.	BB.	ERA.
1947	Butler	Mid. Atl.	24	157	13	4	.765	151	86	67	114	58	3.84
1948	Norfolk	Pied.	30	216	16	8	.667	182	83	62	*171	113	2.58
1949	Binghamton	East.	26	168	16	5	.762	118	38	30	*151	54	*1.61
1950	Kansas City	A. A.	12	95	6	3	.667	81	39	34	80	48	3.22
1950	New York	Amer.	20	112	9	1	.900	87	39	35	59	52	2.81
1951–52							(In Military Service)						
1953	New York	Amer.	32	207	18	6	.750	187	77	69	110	110	3.00
1954	New York	Amer.	34	211	16	8	.667	170	72	66	125	101	2.82
1955	New York	Amer.	39	254	*18	7	.720	188	83	74	137	113	2.62
1956	New York	Amer.	31	226	19	6	*.760	187	70	62	141	84	*2.47
1957	New York	Amer.	24	129	11	5	.688	114	46	37	84	53	2.58
1958	New York	Amer.	30	219	14	7	.667	174	62	49	145	62	*2.01
1959	New York	Amer.	35	204	16	10	.615	194	82	69	114	89	3.04
1960	New York	Amer.	33	193	12	9	.571	168	76	66	85	65	3.08

YEAR	CLUB	LEAGUE	G	IP	W	L	PCT	H	R	ER	SO	BB	ERA
1963	New York	Amer.	38	*269	*24	7	*.774	240	94	82	189	56	2.74
1964	New York	Amer.	39	245	17	6	.739	212	67	58	172	57	2.13
1965	New York	Amer.	37	244	16	13	.552	241	97	88	162	50	3.25
1966	New York †	Amer.	22	73	2	5	.286	79	33	20	43	24	2.47
1967	New York ‡	Amer.	7	44	2	4	.333	40	11	8	21	9	1.64
	Major League Totals		498	3171	236	106	.690	2766	1107	967	1956	1086	2.74

† Underwent operation for circulatory blockage in left shoulder; on disabled list from August 22 through end of season.
‡ Retired on May 30.

WORLD SERIES RECORD

YEAR	CLUB	LEAGUE	G	IP	W	L	PCT	H	R	ER	SO	BB	ERA
1950	New York	Amer.	1	8⅔	1	0	1.000	7	2	0	7	1	0.00
1953	New York	Amer.	2	8	0	1	.000	9	4	4	7	2	4.50
1955	New York	Amer.	2	17	2	0	1.000	13	6	4	10	8	2.12
1956	New York	Amer.	2	12	1	1	.500	14	8	7	8	2	5.25
1957	New York	Amer.	2	16	1	0	.500	11	2	2	7	5	1.13
1958	New York	Amer.	3	15⅓	0	1	.000	19	8	7	16	5	4.11
1960	New York	Amer.	2	18	2	0	1.000	11	0	0	8	2	0.00
1961	New York	Amer.	2	14	2	0	1.000	6	0	0	7	1	0.00
1962	New York	Amer.	3	19⅔	1	1	.500	24	9	9	12	4	4.12
1963	New York	Amer.	2	12	0	2	.000	10	7	6	8	3	4.50
1964	New York	Amer.	1	5⅓	0	1	.000	8	5	5	4	1	8.44
	World Series Totals		22	146	10	8	.556	132	51	44	94	34	2.71

ALL-STAR GAME RECORD

YEAR	LEAGUE	IP	W	L	PCT	H	R	ER	SO	BB	ERA
1954	American	3	0	0	.000	1	0	0	0	1	0.00
1955	American	1⅔	0	0	.000	5	5	3	0	1	16.20
1956	American	1	0	0	.000	3	2	2	2	1	18.00
1959	American (first game)	⅓	0	1	.000	3	2	2	0	0	54.00
1960	American (second game)	3	0	1	.000	5	3	3	1	0	9.00
1961	American (first game)	3	0	0	.000	2	1	1	2	0	3.00
	All-Star Game Totals	12	0	2	.000	19	13	11	5	3	8.25

Scout and Minor League Pitching Coach, New York Yankees, May 30, 1967 through end of season; Coach, New York Yankees, 1968.

Courtesy of the 1968 Baseball Register, published by The Sporting News, St. Louis, Mo.

MICKEY CHARLES MANTLE

Born October 20, 1931, at Spavinaw, Okla.
Height, 6.00. Weight, 201.
Threw right and batted left and righthanded.
Hobby—Hunting.

Established following major league records: Most consecutive home runs in two games (4), July 4 and July 6, 1961; most years 100 or more strikeouts, season (8), 1967; most strikeouts, lifetime (1710), 1968; most home runs, six consecutive games (8), June 28 through July 3, 1966. Tied following major league records: Most consecutive home runs in times at bat (4), July 4, final two appearances and July 6, first two appearances; hit home runs in all parks, 1964.

Tied American League record for most consecutive years leading in strikeouts (3), 1960.

Led American League in walks with 113 in 1955, 146 in 1957, 129 in 1958, 126 in 1961 and 122 in 1962; led league batters in strikeouts with 107 in 1954, 126 in 1959 and 125 in 1960 and tied for lead with 111 in 1952 and 120 in 1958; led league in total bases with 376 in 1956; 207 in 1958 and 294 in 1960; led league in slugging percentage with .611 in 1955, .705 in 1956, .687 in 1961 and .605 in 1962; tied for league lead in double plays by outfielder with 5 in 1952.

Hit three home runs in a game, May 13, 1955.
Won American League Triple Crown, 1956.
Named Most Valuable Player, American League, 1956–57–62.
Named Outstanding American League player by The Sporting News, 1956–62.
Named Major League Player of the Year by The Sporting News, 1956.
Named as outfielder on The Sporting News' All-Star Major League Teams, 1952–56–57.
Named as outfielder on The Sporting News' American League All-Star Team, 1961–62–64.
Received Gold Glove award as outstanding fielding outfielder in American League, 1962.

YEAR	CLUB	LEAGUE	POS.	G.	AB.	R.	H.	2B.	3B.	HR.	RBI.	B.A.	PO.	A.	E.	F.A.
1949	Independence	K-O-M	SS	89	323	54	101	15	7	7	63	.313	121	245	47	.886
1950	Joplin	W. A.	SS	137	519	*141	*199	30	12	26	136	*.383	202	340	55	.908
1951	New York	Amer.	OF	96	341	61	91	11	5	13	65	.267	135	4	6	.959
1951	Kansas City	A. A.	OF	40	166	32	60	9	3	11	50	.361	110	4	4	.966
1952	New York	Am.	*OF-3B	142	549	94	171	37	7	23	87	.311	348	16	*14	.963
1953	New York	Am.	OF-SS	127	461	105	136	24	3	21	92	.295	322	10	6	.982
1954	New York	Am.	*OF-IF	146	543	*129	163	17	12	27	102	.300	334	*25	9	.976
1955	New York	Am.	OF-SS	147	517	121	153	25	*11	*37	99	.306	376	11	2	.995
1956	New York	Amer.	OF	150	533	*132	188	22	5	*52	*130	*.353	370	10	4	.990
1957	New York	Amer.	OF	144	474	*121	173	28	6	34	94	.365	324	6	7	.979
1958	New York	Amer.	OF	150	519	*127	158	21	1	*42	97	.304	331	5	8	.977
1959	New York	Amer.	OF	144	541	104	154	23	4	31	75	.285	366	7	2	*.995
1960	New York	Amer.	OF	153	527	*119	145	17	6	*40	94	.275	326	9	3	.991
1961	New York	Amer.	OF	153	514	*132	163	16	6	54	128	.317	351	6	6	.983
1962	New York	Amer.	OF	123	377	96	121	15	1	30	89	.321	214	4	5	.978
1963	New York	Amer.	OF	65	172	40	54	8	0	15	35	.314	99	2	1	.990
1964	New York	Amer.	OF	143	465	92	141	25	2	35	111	.303	217	3	5	.978
1965	New York	Amer.	OF	122	361	44	92	12	1	19	46	.255	165	3	6	.966
1966	New York	Amer.	OF	108	333	40	96	12	1	23	56	.286	172	2	0	1.000
1967	New York	Amer.	1B	144	440	63	108	17	0	22	55	.245	1089	91	8	.993

WORLD SERIES RECORD

Hit home run with bases full in World Series game, third inning, October 4, 1953.

Holds following World Series lifetime records: Most home runs (18), most runs scored (42), most runs batted in (40), most total bases (123), most long hits (26), most extra bases on long hits (64), most bases on balls (43), most strikeouts (54), most Series played by outfielder (12), and most games played by an outfielder (63).

Tied following World Series records: Most consecutive strikeouts, Series, 5, 1953; Most errors by outfielder, seven-game Series, 2, 1964; Most runs batted in, inning, 4, October 4, 1953; Most hits, game, 4, October 8, 1960 and Most runs seven-game Series, 8, 1960 and 1964.

YEAR	CLUB	LEAGUE	POS.	G.	AB.	R.	H.	2B.	3B.	HR.	RBI.	B.A.	PO.	A.	E.	F.A.
1951	New York †	Amer.	OF	2	5	1	1	0	0	0	0	.200	4	0	0	1.000
1952	New York	Amer.	OF	7	29	5	10	1	1	2	3	.345	16	0	0	1.000
1953	New York	Amer.	OF	6	24	3	5	0	0	2	7	.208	14	0	0	1.000
1955	New York	Am.	OF-PH	3	10	1	2	0	0	1	1	.200	4	1	0	1.000
1956	New York	Amer.	OF	7	24	6	6	1	0	3	4	.250	18	0	0	1.000
1957	New York	Am.	OF-PH	6	19	3	5	0	0	1	2	.263	8	0	1	.889
1958	New York	Amer.	OF	7	24	4	6	0	1	2	3	.250	16	0	0	1.000
1960	New York	Amer.	OF	7	25	8	10	1	0	3	11	.400	15	0	0	1.000
1961	New York	Amer.	OF	2	6	0	1	0	0	0	0	.167	2	0	0	1.000
1962	New York	Amer.	OF	7	25	2	3	1	0	0	0	.120	11	0	0	1.000
1963	New York	Amer.	OF	4	15	1	2	0	0	1	1	.133	6	0	0	1.000
1964	New York	Amer.	OF	7	24	8	8	2	0	3	8	.333	12	0	2	.857
World Series Totals				65	230	42	59	6	2	18	40	.257	126	1	3	.977

† Injured right knee in fifth inning of second game; did not play for rest of Series.

ALL-STAR GAME RECORD

YEAR	LEAGUE	POS.	AB.	R.	H.	2B.	3B.	HR.	RBI.	B.A.	PO.	A.	E.	F.A.
1953	American	OF	2	0	0	0	0	0	0	.000	0	0	0	.000
1954	American	OF	5	1	2	0	0	0	0	.400	2	0	0	1.000
1955	American	OF	6	1	2	0	0	1	3	.333	3	0	0	1.000
1956	American	OF	4	1	1	0	0	0	1	.250	0	0	0	.000
1957	American	OF	4	1	1	0	0	0	0	.250	4	0	0	1.000
1958	American	OF	2	0	1	0	0	0	0	.500	3	0	0	1.000
1959	American (both games)	OF	3	0	1	0	0	0	0	.333	3	0	0	1.000
1960	American (both games)	OF	4	0	1	0	0	0	0	.250	5	0	0	1.000
1961	American (both games)	OF	6	0	0	0	0	0	0	.000	5	0	0	1.000
1962	American (first game)	OF	1	0	0	0	0	0	0	.000	2	0	0	1.000
1964	American	OF	4	1	1	0	0	0	0	.250	0	0	0	1.000
1967	American	PH	1	0	0	0	0	0	0	.000	0	0	0	.000
1968	American	PH	1	0	0	0	0	0	0	.000	0	0	0	.000
All-Star Game Totals			43	5	10	0	0	2	4	.233	27	0	0	1.000

Member of American League All-Star team in 1952 and 1962 (second game); did not play. Named to American League All-Star team for 1963 and 1965 games; replaced due to injury.

Courtesy of the 1969 Baseball Register, published by The Sporting News, St. Louis, Mo.